THE
BLACK
SITUATION

THE
BLACK
SITUATION

by ADDISON GAYLE, JR.

HORIZON PRESS   NEW YORK

ACKNOWLEDGMENTS

The author thanks the following publications in which some of the articles (here in somewhat altered form) originally appeared: *Amistad, Journal of Human Relations, Liberator, Long Island University Urban Studies Symposium, Negro Digest, Repartee, Rights and Reviews.*

FOR MY WIFE

CONTENTS

"Every man is a mad man; but what is a human destiny for if not to unite the mad man with the universe."

—ANDRÉ MALRAUX

"I have told you my truth, and now you may tell me yours."

—FRIEDRICH NIETZSCHE

THE SON OF

MY FATHER

I AM COMPELLED to state here, in the beginning, that the thoughts recorded in this book are mine alone and that I do not, nor have I attempted, to speak for any other black man in American Society. I make this statement in the hope of sparing some other Negro the moments of frustration and anger which I experience when some "Negro Leader" on television, bright lights illuminating his unscarred countenance, proceeds to tell America in impassioned tones what I think, believe, and want.

Such utterances by Negro Leaders have produced severe traumas for me; causing me to hurl notebook, pen, and pencil at my television set, shout obscenities at the unhearing figure before me; and finally, not too long ago, when I had almost reached the breaking point, I scribbled a note to one of these leaders asking that on future occasions he preface his remarks by stating that: "I speak for every Negro in America, except Addison Gayle." The letter accomplished nothing, for three weeks ago this same leader was on television again, informing the public that he, not other Negro Leaders, spoke for me.

America is at that desperate stage when, feeling the threat from her long neglected citizenry, she needs some supporting, sustaining voice to assure her that the neglected are still, despite all, hopeful, passive, and restrained. Nations, like men, are wary of truth, for truth is too often not beautiful, as Keats believed, but very painful and very discomforting. It is not comforting to be reminded that those who sow the wind shall reap the whirlwind, not even when the whirlwind appears so visibly, as in frequent summers of discontent when desperate men have belied the vocal protestations of their leaders.

No Negro in America speaks for me; neither do I speak for any one else. It would, perhaps, be too great a shock to find compatibility between my thoughts and those of others; for unlike Narcissus, a mirror image would cause me untold discomfort. I am, I know, a desperate man, a cynical man and, perhaps, according to Freudian psychology which can in no way explain me, a sick man. Some of my friends would add, quickly, a mad man. I do not object. Perhaps to be sane in this society is the best evidence of insanity. To repress all that I know, to keep hidden in my subconscious all that I feel may inevitably force me to those acts of desperation which I am capable of viewing here, frankly and honestly with a certain objective detachment.

This is to say that the very act of recording these thoughts may provide that catharsis which will enable me to retain control of that demon within my breast which allows me no respite in twentieth century America. One wonders what fate might have befallen Dostoyevsky had he not created Roskolnikov or Demitri? What might Baldwin have become, had he not been capable of traducing Bigger Thomas in print? And Wright, Bigger's creator, what might he have been were not the fearful portrait of Bigger etched upon his subconscious mind, displayed upon that canvas of the psyche in garish, brutal colors?

The end product of writing should be revelation for both the writer and reader. I have no quarrel with those who argue that poetry "should not mean but be": I simply call them liars, and let it go at that. I hold no breach against those who argue that Black literature, in the main, has not conformed to those artistic rules and canons established by the academicians. I know that such tools are important to them. For they are incapable of understanding Black literature without the aid of these instruments of dissection with which they are most dexterous.

Literature, however, and Black literature in particular, should afford revelation and insight into truth when created under conditions favorable to free, honest expression. For the Afro-American, solitude is the most necessary condition; for Blacks are abominable liars, especially, in those cases where an audience is concerned. This is not to suggest that black writers are not also liars —indeed a great many are the most notorious liars of all. But, alone, secreted only with his thoughts and a desire to honestly record those thoughts, the black writer may, at least, blunder into an awareness of truth.

This truth, then, will come as a revelation; and I have little doubt that mine will—especially to those who, over the years, have professed to "know" me. They will discover, sometimes painfully, that they have not known me at all; yet, this is primarily because I have not known myself. For example, I did not know —or would not admit, which is the same thing—how vehement was my hatred even toward those whom I professed to love most passionately.

If however, those who remember me will recall my unspoken nuances—the quick bowing of my head, the slight raising of my eyebrows, the smile which has never really been a smile, the uncomfortable habit that I have of moving from place to place whenever alone in a room with white people—then they can begin to piece together the puzzle of our relationship, and to make some sense out of what I write here. When I say that I hated, I am uttering my first verbal truth with full cognizance of its import; and if not a revelation to others, this is indeed, a revelation to me. This is my first positive statement to white people; and because it is the truth, I do not apologize for it. I only regret that I did not, or could not, make it before.

Perhaps I did not really hate before! Perhaps, despite everything, I retained enough of my mother's Christian preachments to think of love as the universal solvent, the cleansing cream which America need but apply to the ugly, pockmarked blemishes upon its white-hued surface. Perhaps I believed that one could not create a world of hatred because invariably that world became a suspicious one, an isolated one; and, finally, one so infected by disease that life, any life, trapped within it was worthless. Or, perhaps, I was too much of a coward to hate: too timid, too meek.

And this despite the fact that I owe what some people call my success to hatred. Six years ago I worked as a porter at a government establishment in Brooklyn, New York. After four years, I left that job and three days later began to assault the pavements of New York City searching for another. My odyssey began early on a Monday morning, on a dismal, overcast day in May when the streets of New York seemed most indifferent—a day much like those which I had cherished in the Virginia town where I was born.

Long before, on such days, I had searched for jobs in Virginia with less trepidation, with less overt fear than that which plagued me as I searched for employment in New York City. To state for the nth time that the Afro-American's life in the South in comparison with his life in the North is in many ways more comfortable if not more compatible is to state what is general knowledge. For there is comfort in honesty, in knowing that the perils one faces are blatantly visible, not cloaked with the time-honored garb of hypocrisy and deceit. The South is nothing if not honest, and Blacks who hate it the most, grudgingly admit to its honesty.

The indictment against the North, however, stems from its dishonesty, its hypocritical facade which has engendered more frustration in the black intellectual than all the perverted acts perpetrated upon Negroes by those creatures who inhabit the hinterlands of the South. In the South, the Negro is, when visible, merely a Negro, an accursed son of Ham destined, like a mute, to be the stanchion of stubborn support for a romantic, idyllic utopia where class and race are so structured as to allow for a well-ordered society. Here, only the Blacks speak of equality. The whites hurl the correlative word, "place"; for there is a place for the Negro in Southern society: albeit, a place at the bottom of a rotten cesspool—yet a place where being black, though a stigma, is legitimate. The Negroes are still considered as a people and brotherhood means loyalty to one's own race.

In the North, on the other hand, the Negro is conceived of as an instrument, a non-being, the noble savage, who must, in whatever way possible, be civilized; scrubbed clean of his heredity; robbed of his propensity for blackness, the last vestige of tribalism erased from his mind. Like the missionary, the Northern white seeks to bring the savage within the confines of Western Civilization with far more potent weapons than guns and bibles: higher horizons programs, civil rights commissions, urban renewal, and cultural centers for black youth.

There is more truth in the South than in the North, more honest feeling in the man who knots the rope about your neck, more honest conviction in the mob which howls for your blood. In the North one falls into that absurd world where impotent men gather unto themselves other men as children, intent on guiding them, on leading them to that coming paradise, that enchanted land of freedom and equality, not withstanding the fact that paradise is only paradise if one finds it himself.

Here in the North, rhetoric and practice come into conflict: It is no surprise that the great rhetoricians of America are Northerners, for here rhetoric is the most celebrated avocation. From the politician in the highest echelons of Government to the freshman college student come the wail of discontent, the table thumping oratory, the endless reports of committees, civil rights groups, civic organizations, all attesting to the deep concern, the great sympathy felt by men of the North, more sophisticated, more liberal, for their fellow citizens who happen to be black.

Such people believe their own rhetoric; and it is their rhetoric which sustains them. They conceive of rhetoric and practice as one and the same. The college chairman who heads a committee to improve conditions in the ghetto, and yet neglects to improve the conditions in his college so that more ghetto residents may attend, is equating rhetoric with practice. The politician who, although voting for civil rights bills, cautions Afro-Americans not to move too fast is equating rhetoric with practice. The college student who demands tolerance from others toward Blacks and neglects to make such demands upon his parents and neighbors is equating rhetoric with practice.

The Negro, therefore, recognizing the conflict, capable of differentiating between rhetoric and practice, yet unable to divine the motives for the great disparities which he knows to exist, is incapable of finding a bearing, a central point in an absurd world where men are victims of their own rhetoric. It is the frustrations engendered by such conflicts which drive black people to acts of frustrations, to acts of violence, ofttimes, as in the case of a friend, to suicide.

The Negro, the world's greatest dissimulator, is unable to survive in a world where dissimulation is the norm, hypocrisy the accustomed and accepted mode of behavior. Better to be entrapped in a web of practicality where men take the word "place" as the God-ordained condition of twenty-five million people than to be enmeshed in a web where men are convinced that their manifest destiny lies in mesmerizing the natives by their spell-binding, hypnotic oratory. The first web can be cut; its strands can be severed; at the least, men never tire of attempting to rip it apart. The second web, however, is non-corporeal, having no body, no structure, no substance. It is impervious to assault, except that of the most violent nature; for the Messiah is incapable of differentiating between rhetoric and practice until such time as those who see truth in men's actions, not in their words, nail him, shamelessly and without guilt, to the cross.

It is not long before the Negro who journeys from South to North is called witness to his moment of truth. Epiphanies are almost daily occurrences. There is so much to be revealed. There are so many thousands of shapes, forms and symbols through which revelation may come. The first epiphany often occurs in the North when the Negro first faces his hoped-for-employer. Contrary to most reports, on first arriving in the North, the Southern Black is not incensed by the ghetto—this comes later—for the Northern ghetto has always held mystical, romantic connotations for him. Here it is that the tenuous tie with the North, perfected through the years by the mass exodus of his ancestors, is most secure. Few Blacks in the South have neither friends nor relatives in Northern ghettoes. Thus, neither the filth and stench of the ghetto, nor its chronic violence can rid the newcomer of that compulsion to dwell among his own in the Harlems, Wattses, Houghs and Bedford Stuyvesants of the North.

Discrimination, northern style, is encountered when the newcomer searches for his first job and is brought face to face with his first northern employer. The encounter is more likely than not to be traumatic, reenforcing the subdued antagonism engendered by the South, intensifying it to the point wherein this antagonism gives way to a hatred which given birth, feeds upon itself like a cancerous cell until the victim is either consumed or miraculously made whole—himself consuming that which would destroy him.

Early in the morning on that dark overcast day, I checked out five jobs, all of which had surreptitiously vanished before I arrived. My sixth stop was the corner of Delancey Street and Broadway, a combination restaurant and newsstand which, according to the New York Times, "Wanted: a man to do light portering, some clerking." It was the "light portering" which caused me to be hopeful, for such job descriptions in the South are usually synonyms for Negroes.

I was met at the door of the shop by a dark-hued white man who, mistaking me for a customer, commented on the state of the weather. Smiling, I proceeded to point out the true nature of my business which was not to buy wares but instead to sell my labor. No sooner had I mentioned the ad than the man abruptly turned his back to me, and walked quickly to the other end of the store, informing me through a running monologue with himself that the job was taken. However, his actions, not his words, convinced me that he was lying. All morning I had been turned away from jobs, always with a smile, a sympathetic murmur of sympathy, unbelievable to be sure, yet unchallengeable on any save intuitive grounds.

This man had made it impossible for me to believe him. I left the store, went across the street to a drugstore, waited a few minutes, and dialed the number listed in the newspaper. The man himself answered the telephone. Mimicking James Mason, I asked if the job listed in the morning paper had been filled. The answer was no. I asked if I could come over to see about the job. I was told to come at once. I went to the store a second time. This time the man met me, rage breathing from every pore of his nostrils, his ugly face contorted into the most weird design.

"Yes?" He growled.

"I came for the job." I announced.

"There ain't no job!" He replied.

"I just called, and you said there was one," I answered, "You said come right over."

Briefly, a flicker of surprise came to his eyes, but he recovered quickly. "You didn't call here," he said; "that's a lie, there ain't no job." He turned on his heels and went to serve a customer who had come in.

I stared after him for a few minutes before finally walking out of the store. There was a big lump in my stomach. My hands shook noticeably. In facing him with what I knew to be the truth, in forcing him to acknowledge his own lie, I had, perhaps, scored a moral victory. Yet I was still without a job because a man who did not know me, had decided *a priori* that I should not have one. The moral victory was far less sustaining than my growing hatred.

Floyd Patterson, in his first fight with Ingemar Johanssen, was knocked to the canvas again and again, only to rise yet another time. Many were awed by the tenacious courage displayed by the champion, the refusal to stay down, to say die. I was not amazed; for I too had learned early to absorb merciless punishment, to pick myself up from the canvas of a ring in which the fight can only end in life or death.

Like the ex-heavyweight champion, I was on my feet searching for another job less than fifteen minutes after absorbing a crushing blow to my psyche. This time I intended to shape the odds nearer to my liking. I decided to buy a job.

The headquarters of the job-buying market is a narrow street at the southern tip of Manhattan, some few feet from the Hudson River. On this narrow street, occupying an entire block, are an assortment of dilapidated office buildings housing numerous agencies which legally traffic in human flesh. Sometimes as many as five agencies are in one single building. Each agency occupies a large room, two at the most, partitioned into two sections. One section, the larger is usually, though not always, furnished with folding chairs; in the other section, beyond the partition, neat, middle-aged businessmen (white) and their assistants sit at wooden desks surrounded by telephones.

Throughout the day, from opening time at eight o'clock in the morning to closing time at five o'clock at night, people of all races come to these partitioned offices offering themselves as saleable commodities. On any given day, one will find a small number of white applicants, a large number of Puerto Rican applicants, and a great number of black applicants.

I chose one of the smaller agencies which had emptied, somewhat, at that hour of the day. A number of people were still present. Some were waiting, I suppose, for clarification of job offers. Some women were checking to see if the prospects for domestic work tomorrow were brighter than prospects today. Standing along the two walls of the agency were older Negro men, in whose faces the tragedy of a people was stenciled in bold, heavy lines, watching each new arrival suspiciously, their ears attuned to the ring of the telephone; they smiled condescendingly each time the eyes of the agent swept their paths; for the agent was their savior, able to reward them with a half day's work, enabling them to fight off the D.T.'s, hunger, or eviction yet a little while longer.

I was met by an assistant, a charming, brownskinned girl of about twenty-one, heavily rouged, her hair in a pompadour, her false eyelashes flickering as if in amusement. We smiled at one another; and she communicated her nervousness by smoking her cigarette almost to the filter, leaving her long fingers stained a deeper brown than her skin. Like me, she too lived at a fever pitch of desperation; though she, like some omniscient spectator of Dante's Hell, watched men, women, and sometimes teenage children stacked before her eyes, no longer human, but instead objects to be auctioned away for one week's salary—the legal requirements of the agency. She had dwelled among these hollow men and women so long, these mechanical men and women of Kafka's novels, that she had become almost hollow and mechanical herself. I pitied her, even as she pitied me.

She helped me to fill out several forms, and after I had completed them, she motioned me to a folding chair, took the forms, and deposited them on the desk of a short, fat white man, whose bald head seemed a comic distraction in this place where laughter would have been an unforgivable crime.

Not too long after, I sat in a chair at the desk, staring at the man's bald head, listening to him describe a job recently referred to his agency. The job was located in a restaurant on Broadway, two blocks from City Hall. The prerequisites were for a young man who had some experience at handling a cash register, and who would not balk at long hours. I satisfied the agent that I met all the requirements, after which he brought out a number of papers upon which I scribbled my signature. The assistant gave me a card bearing the agency's letterhead and the name of the man I was to see, and smiled at me knowingly; I quickly left that little room, which smelled like something akin to death.

The restaurant was located in the basement of a large hotel which, at that time, was undergoing alteration. I passed several black workers: plasterers, hod-carriers, and porters, one of whom pointed the way to the manager at the door of the office—he, seeing me approaching, had come from behind a glass enclosure. He was young, blond, his face clean of blemishes, his body thin, athletic in appearance. His movements seemed impetuous, quick, and determined. I handed him the agent's card.

Hardly had he finished reading the card, before, without hesitation, almost as if I were not present, he blurted out: "But why did they send you? We don't hire Negroes."

We recoiled one from the other! He because he had said what he did; I because he had said it so blatantly. He was, I suppose, an honest man, and instinctively, he uttered the truth which needed no supporting rationale. I never thought for a moment that he hated me, nor that he thought much about me at all; this was not necessary to justify the irrefutable statement: "We don't hire Negroes."

It was the look of consternation on my face which made him offer me carfare, which prompted him to tell me that he was sorry. He looked after me with sympathetic eyes, as I, having spurned his offer of carfare, backed away as one fighting to sleep through some horrible nightmare. I walked away, almost in a state of shock. In this shocked state, I telephoned the agency, reported what had happened, hung up the phone, and boarded the "A" train for Brooklyn.

When finally I reached my stop in the heart of Bedford-Stuyvesant, the ghetto to which I came now for some solace, for some semblance of myself, some testament of myself as a human being, I left the subway, bypassing the bars along the way, where

I would find that human misery by which to measure my own. I avoided those who knew me, even at that moment when I wanted their affection the most. I avoided them because I did not want them to see me cry. Crying is an act which one should perform only in private, for crying is a private way of groping for truth. Once inside of my apartment, I removed the phone from the hook, locked my door, fell across the bed, and cried.

On the bed, clawing and clutching at the pillows, my breath coming in quick, short gasps, my nose filled with mucus, my mouth hot, dry. I twisted, shouted, and screamed almost in convulsion; the tears gushing from my eyes; my body burning as if seared by some scorching, burning flame; with my fists I flailed the pillows; with my fingernails I tore at my hair, drew blood from my skin; like some hurt, wounded beast in orgasm. I surrendered my soul to that Faustian devil who hovers over the black male, in pain, in ecstasy, in total to complete, everlasting hatred.

In time I would come to understand that it was not only the acts of discrimination; not only the feelings of rejection; not only the soul-rending words, "We don't hire Negroes"; but, instead, the motivation for the surrender to Mephistopheles was simply that white men had made me cry, had forced me to that point where I would seek a baptism in my own tears; a baptism which would cleanse me of any sense of responsibility to them, any sense of affection for them, any sense of respect for them. The ultimate pain which any man can inflict upon another is to force him to tears.

"God gave Noah the rainbow sign/No more water, the fire next time," chanted a now forgotten black slave. For me the water had come to give birth to that fire which would consume me, almost completely. Sparks from this fire propelled me to college, forced me to attempt, naively, to wreak vengeance upon those who had forced me to reveal my soul in all of its nakedness. Instructors who knew me as a conscientious, hardworking student had no cognizance of that demon within which forced me on; nor could they know that the mere sight of them, their whiteness, was enough to trigger that demon into action. Riding the wings of the demon, I pushed my way through curricula foreign to me, spent entire nights writing and rewriting term papers; stood Buddha-like as my instructors attempted to convince me of their dedication to the human spirit.

Some were kind enough to single me out, to invite me to their homes. They questioned me about my hopes, my expectations, and about race relations. Always, I lied to them; partly out of fear, but partly, too, out of the belief that were I to tell them the truth, to relate even one tenth of my truth, they would expel me from school and have me locked up in the nearest hospital for the mentally insane.

Others spoke of me in laudatory terms: They told me that I was the kind of Negro whom they would "not mind living next door to them"; that I should be a "spokesman for my people"; that I was proving that any man with initiative could prosper in this democracy. They refused to see me as other than a phenomenon, a testament to all that their rhetoric had portrayed. I was the emancipated Negro, shrived of the sin of blackness because I had proven that I could absorb the wisdom of Shakespeare, Plato, and Emerson. I was the transformed savage, having been rescued from the jungle of the ghetto and stripped of the ghetto facade; now I was almost human, ready to be welcomed, even if halfheartedly—for the savage can never be completely transformed—into middle class senility, impotence, and death.

Students, on the other hand, were worse than instructors. If the instructors believed me to be intellectually resurrected, the students considered me to be socially resurrected, capable now of association on an almost equal level with them. I was *the Negro* to have at social gatherings. I avoided most of these and went only when I was bored with school work. I was the Negro who talked on their terms, voiced their discontents, and gave words to their frustration.

To them I told as much of the truth as possible, until I discovered that they sought this truth, eagerly, masochistically, as authoritative evidence, facts from the donkey's mouth, with which to substantiate the everchanging tenor of their own rhetoric. To be sure, they dreamed of the new Canaan, but one from which I, as an individual, would be excluded. When I entered their new world, I would enter as mind, as intellect, divested of that corporeal form, body, bedecked by a black skin. Believing in the power of rationality, these students saw me in terms of intellect only; for to them intellect was unlimited. I, however, could not live by intellect and intellect alone; for there was, within my breast, an irrational demon which often propelled me to irrational acts. I could not, therefore, accept their compact, for unfortunately, sometime ago, I had signed the most binding compact of all.

"I fall upon the thorns of life," wrote Shelley, "I bleed!" And sometimes one wishes that the bleeding would be over and done with; and if not this, then that some tourniquet might be applied to stop the flowing blood once and for all. On the other hand, perhaps it would be best if the blood gushed profusely, like a water hose, pushing out the impurities quickly, allowing one only the intoxicating moment of release, an ecstatic descent into a dream world, where there is no life, and thus, no pain.

"Verweile doch, du bist so schön," she called after me. Standing by the plane, tall, slender, deep blue eyes, blonde hair cut short about her neck, tears in her eyes, she watched as I walked slowly, unsteadily up the ramp. The fleeting hour was fleeting all too quickly, and never again would we see one another, never again walk the same sandy beach together; never again share the same world.

Her world had been as strange to me as my world was to her. Few of us, like Malcolm X, make the trip to Mecca where one meets people of different skin color whom one cannot reject outright. Yet many Negroes find their personal Meccas; and there, though color is never irrelevant, there is perhaps something better —one is indifferent to color.

She was my Mecca. Here color was not negated, but simply ignored. Together we found the new Canaan, and yet, I knew that I could not live in it. Too many Blacks were outside, too many Blacks whose tortured faces continued to move before my mind like so many accusing mouths; and we both knew that one day, I would have to acquiesce to the painful utterances of those mouths, desert Canaan, and return to the ghetto not, as my father had hoped, to save the people, but to die with them.

We arrived, therefore, at some definition of our life together, found some way of memorializing all that had been, and we stumbled upon the concept of the fleeting hour (die fliegende Stunde).

"Verweile doch, du bist so schön," we chanted night after night together (remain, so fair thou art), for fair those hours were indeed. Two human beings caught in a historic trap, one incapable of destroying a vicious, binding compact, desiring always to be victim, rather than victimizer; two people living for a short span of time in a peace, a serenity to which no words can give form and body; two lovers who, were there some merciful God, would have been allowed to perish then and there.

It was the hour, however, which would perish; not we. Cowards, we would continue to live, to be hurled again and again upon those sharp, jagged thorns which drained us of life-giving blood. Soon the magic of the words, the spell of the incantation, "verweile doch, du bist so schön," would mean little more than an epigram for an essay or a poem. Like Keats, we had spent our allotted time with the nightingale, drunk of hemlock, and tasted of mirth and flora; and yet even such memories were doomed to death in the atmosphere to which I was compelled to return.

The Negro, I have written elsewhere, is timeless; and this is so, for time stopped for us the moment the good ship *Jesus* unloaded its first cargo in the New World. Since that moment, we have sat atop the jagged thorns of life convulsing, like so many tortured animals, from wounds inflicted by weapons as diverse as whips, pistols, ropes and rhetoric. Yet rhetoric is perhaps the most bludgeoning weapon of all. We have been enslaved anew by rhetoric: that of our own prophets as well as that of the missionaries. We fear our own emotions, seek to check them, to subdue them in obedience to some man-made laws which we should neither respect nor honor.

We have chanted love thine enemy, when every fibre of our being has cried "death" to those who despoil us; we have preached forgiveness, when not even the most pious among us can forgive that brutal past from which we sprang; we have sung hymns to a God who, in his infinite mercy, has forsaken us as readily as he forsook his first son; we have dreamed of "a fleeting hour" when even that was not enough to assuage the wounds of the past. Hollow men, we have not dared consider the admonition of Ralph Ellison's invisible man: ". . . maybe freedom lies in hating."

But if not, perhaps freedom lies in realizing that one hates. Perhaps all that is left the black man in America is a revelation, an awareness of himself; and perhaps the key to that conundrum posed by the black poets, the answer to the question of identity, lies in an exploration of one's true emotions, starting at that elementary first principle of denigrated humanity: "I hate."

I begin this book, cognizant of the war which goes on constantly within my soul. It is a fierce war and, no doubt, a destructive one. Yet this war must be fought out to some conclusion before I can begin to wrestle with the problems of men in general. That things which have happened to me, have happened also to others, I have little doubt; yet in happening to me, they have left wounds upon my psyche, and pain others cannot imagine.

I am, I suppose, a stranger; one who has sought a personal truth, hoping to be more enlightened by it than his audience; a stranger, who believes that men live always with some demon within their breasts which can only be exorcised by a dedication to those frightening realities which exist at the moment; a stranger, who has always believed that mankind would be better off today had it accepted as savior the choice of that mob which shouted "Give us Barabbas," instead of accepting one who, from the cross, could only issue his pitiable, feeble moan: "Father forgive them, for they know not what they do."

I ENDURED

IN 1966 at the commencement exercises of the University of California, attired in black cap and gown, tassel pushed to the right, I arose at the deep-throated command, voiced by a tired, bored chancellor—"Masters of Arts, arise!" Slowly, almost unbelievingly, I had arisen with the other recipients of the Master's degree to the applause of guests, parents, students, and faculty members.

The distance between this step and the first, taken six years before, seemed, then, more than a thousand miles. Set down with others of black skin, in the jungle of the ghetto, I had been expected, to paraphrase James Baldwin, to perish. I had not. I had travelled the thousand miles; and perhaps I should have felt elated.

Perhaps! But if so, the elation did not come. Maybe the company of my fellow graduates had something to do with this. I discovered, then, that I did not like their company; perhaps this had always been so, but now I felt my discomfort more than ever. Most of the graduates were white; and those who were black seemed black in skin color only: they seemed, as Richard Wright once remarked to an African, "to be more Anglo-Saxon than the Anglo-Saxons." To these graduates, the ceremony had meaning, it proved something to them about themselves. They had joined the elite of the nation, and become numbered among the chosen few of the world who had completed five or more years of college, who had survived the ascent to the top of the ivory tower.

Out there stood a world, waiting for them. "I have a world about me," wrote Wordsworth in the "Prelude"; "It is my own, I made it." My fellow students did not have to make their world, they had only to fit in, to become a part of one already in existence. They were blessed, for the making of worlds can be a frustrating experience; thus most men forego the frustration and settle for the world as it is.

Yet, for Blacks in general, and for me in particular, this entailed settling for a world made by others. It meant dwelling forever in the house of the magic mirrors, having distortions flashed upon your mind so often that soon the only reality you knew was that contained in the mirrors. Tennyson has his lady of Shalott lament, shortly before viewing Camelot from her isolated castle for the first time in twelve years: "I am half sick of shadows." But the lady had only lived in her castle for twelve years; suppose she had lived there for a lifetime, knowing nothing but shadows, would she have been able even to recognize Camelot, let alone look down upon it?

"Congratulations," the girl beside me remarked, as once again we took our seats. I smiled and turned away. The program called for more speeches, more music, and more applause: the band was to play a selection from Brahms, the president of the graduating class was to speak on "The Future of the College Graduate." I sat and smiled for a long time until, quite suddenly, the smile turned into a short cynical laugh.

"I endured!" I remarked through my laughter. The girl who had spoken before, looked at me strangely; the handsome dark Negro on the other side of me shifted uneasily in his seat. I laughed again, silently, as again the thought came to my mind—"I endured." But then, just as quickly, another thought came to push the first away, and to silence the laughter altogether. *But many perished in the struggle, many more worthy than you!* To how many of us does this thought come, and how many are haunted by it? What does Ivan Karamazov care if ninety-nine babies live, so long as one must die?

There are many who died, but two come readily to mind. Amos, short and black, orphaned at the age of three, possessed an incredible propensity for remembering the most important facts and details. Almost verbatim, he could recall the important points in the fourteenth, fifteenth, and sixteenth Amendments, and if called upon, the dates on which each amendment was ratified. Bernice, black and skinny, with short hair and soft eyes, was a child prodigy who read Dickens at five years of age.

In the summer of 1965, after receiving my Bachelor's degree, I was back in Newport News, Virginia, visiting my family. On one of those frequent trips to the ice cream store with my young sister, I met Amos. Amos looked older than his thirty years. His cheeks were sunken, and there were deep lines carved in his face. His skin, once so beautiful in its blackness, was now ugly and coarse, covered with dust and grime. "Doc Gayle," he said, extending a dirty hand to me. I grasped the hand, returning his hearty greeting. We talked for a while. "I should've left when you did," he repeated over and over, "I sure wished I had left when you did."

Embarrassed, I attempted to convince him that my leaving had not made that much difference. I was lying and he knew it. No, there were no guarantees if one left to go North. One could perish as quickly in the streets and ghettoes of New York as in the ghettoes of Newport News. But he knew that survival for Negroes in this country is mostly a matter of luck; and one is more likely to be lucky up North than down South—at least the chances of lightening striking are better.

Finally we broke away from each other, he, walking in the opposite direction, head down, shoulders bent. Watching him amble out of sight, I remembered that Booker T. Washington, in his autobiography, *Up From Slavery*, had written: "Our greatest danger is that in the great leap from slavery to freedom we may overlook the fact that the masses of us are to live by the production of our hands, and fail to keep in mind that we shall prosper in proportion as we learn to dignify and glorify common labor and put brains and skill into the common occupations of life. . . ."

These "common occupations," agriculture, mechanics, and the domestic services, were to be performed by those who "without strikes and labor wars had tilled [the] fields, cleared [the] forests, built [the] railroads and cities, and brought forth treasures from the bowels of the earth. . . ." In Washington's view working with one's hands was the essential characteristic of a black laborer; and dignity was accorded those who succeed in bringing forth better crops or making better bricks than their neighbors.

Amos could see little dignity in making bricks or tilling fields; and the possibility was that he never would. Dostoyevsky's Grand Inquisitor offered bread to the masses in opposition to the freedom offered by Jesus Christ. But when the Grand Inquisitor was dishing out his bread, Amos was not there. If he could have chosen, he would have chosen the freedom of Christ instead of the bread of the Inquisitor. Yet he could not choose; there were for him only two alternatives: to fly into some nameless future, or stay and go to the shipyard. Against his will, he was to be part of the black waves which constitute that black ocean of men which Booker T. Washington had implored white industrialists to dip their buckets into.

Now, mentally and spiritually, he was dead. What had flashed so brilliantly in him just twelve years ago, was gone, gone beyond recall. He had wanted to be a lawyer, and he could have been one; now he was a laborer, and he didn't want to be. Somewhere in the plight of the black boy who wanted to be a lawyer and the black man who was a laborer against his will, is the awful truth of this country. But, too, it is a testimony to the power of the philosophy of Booker T. Washington which has held sway for so long over the minds of so many Negroes in every walk of life.

Thank God I did not see Bernice, this one time sweetheart of my memories, who had wanted to be an English teacher, who had taught me things about Huck Finn, Pip, and Bigger Thomas that I never learned in high school. But I heard of her fate from the gossip-vine. She had married one year after completing high school, and the next year the babies had begun to come. There had been little Freddie, and a year later, Janet, and two years later the twins, Loretta and Michael. The following year, no babies came, but the husband left, and the next year Bernice was in jail, picked up for shoplifting. *How many perished in the struggle, many more worthy than you?* "Why," shouted Ivan Karamazov, "did the baby have to die?"

One consults the philosophers! There is, to interpret Hegel on a simplistic level, a divine spirit moving through the universe, and those who are in touch with this divine spirit are masters of men. The acorn, to subject Aristotle to the same simplistic interpretation, is destined from birth to be an oak tree. But Man, constantly changing, evolving, creating his essence as he goes through life, comes out of Sartre's "Existentialism." "Man must surpass himself," says Nietzsche's Zarathustra. Where is the right and where is the wrong? Was Amos destined like the acorn? Was Bernice, because she was not in touch with the divine spirit, doomed to die the death of disillusionment and despair? How could either of them have created their essence in a world which would forever deny their existence?

There is a section, "The Parable of the Laws," in Kafka's novel, *The Trial*, in which the protagonist is told the story of a man who came to the court of the laws, waiting to gain entrance. The man is told that he cannot enter at the moment. Thus he waits, finally dying at the feet of the guard in front of the door, which the guard proceeds to shut forever. The man could have entered the door at the right moment; but when was the right moment? The man could not know himself, and there was no one to tell him. Who should have told him? Who was responsible for his knowing? And who is responsible for Amos and Bernice who had to settle, against their will, for one world because the doors of another had been closed to them? Who should have prepared them for that moment when the doors of American society would crack ever so slightly? Where does the responsibility for their death lie?

One's first response is that the responsibility rests with the individual. Lastly it is the individual who must be the arbitrator of his own destiny. It is he who must cut through the jungle of chaos and confusion in which modern man finds himself. For the Negro, this is more true. Living in a Kafkaesque world, where all experiences are magnified out of proportion, where every daily occurrence borders on the grotesque, where communication on any real and meaningful level, even with those closest to him, is impossible, the Negro must seek in the blackness of his own being for his own truth.

"If ever I can say to the fleeting moment," laments Goethe's Faust, "verweile doch, du bist so schön"—remain, so fair thou art—then will the bargain with Mephistopheles be fulfilled. It is the Afro-American, this modern day Faust, who is forever seeking some fleeting moment—when all that this white world represents will no longer menace him, no longer threaten him. But the Negro must break the Faustian pact himself. There is no God standing ready at the call to rescue him. His God died on the day the first black man was enslaved, the very hour the chains were put about the arms and ankles of the first black slave, and the agonizing wail, torn from the slave's throat each time the whip cut into his black flesh, was but the dying wail of his God.

But here, we are far from the kind of responsibility that Booker T. Washington talked about. Washington continues in his "Autobiography": "In this address I said that the whole future of the Negro rested largely upon the question as to whether or not he should make himself, through his skill, intelligence, and character, of such undeniable value to the community in which he lived that the community could not dispense with his presence. I said that any individual who learned to do something better than anybody else—learned to do a common thing in an uncommon manner—had solved his problem, regardless of the color of his skin."

Here we have the origin of the bootstrap philosophy. The individual must make himself. This is his responsibility. He must pull himself up by his own bootstraps. Washington presupposes a hostile environment on the one hand, but on the other, one tolerant enough to recognize merit. There is a point, supposes Washington, at which all men meet; and this point is reached when one man recognizes that his brother too is lost in the wilderness, yet that he is willing to cut his way out, depending only upon his own strength and power. Rugged individualism and the survival of the fittest: and it is common to all men to recognize the fittest.

From Sophocles to Strindberg, men have inwardly cheered the victor. What does it matter to the Roskolnikovs of the world if Napoleon murdered millions of people on his way to fame? What history calls the victor to account? Each Negro is personally responsible, therefore, for making "himself of value to the community." Pull yourself up by your own bootstraps! This statement has been a blessing to those of us who hope to compensate for our own inadequacies. One wants to deny that his success in life, whatever that may be, was due to the fortuitous winds of fate which happened at that lucky moment to be blowing his way.

We want to believe that the "A" we received in English was a reward for brilliance; and we refuse to accept the fact that being the only Negro in a classroom in a predominantly white college, we began with "B" before the class commenced. The fact that the firm for which we work in the sixties turned down Blacks in the fifties is only—we like to believe—because no Negro of our calibre appeared before.

We have endured. We have pulled ourselves up, and the question that runs uppermost through our minds is "Why have other Negroes not done the same?" "Look," said a young Negro chemistry major, "those same slums down there. I lived in them too!" He didn't say it, but the remark was there, in his chest, waiting to burst out: "And I came out of them, why can't they?"

We ask, therefore, why couldn't Amos and Bernice pull themselves out of the slum which was their own minds? The Bootstrap Philosophy presupposes at the outset that one has boots. And in a metaphorical sense these boots are character, intelligence and skill. But these are not inherited; they are acquired, and once acquired they must be developed. Thus our question now: Who is responsible for the development of these characteristics, granting that they have been acquired?

One argues that it is the family, perhaps because the black family has been made the scapegoat for the ills of Negroes. Every mother and father is responsible for his children, and upon them initially rests the responsibility for the development and growth of the child. (One's mind, however, runs off into all kinds of analogies. One thinks of the American Constitution and one supposes that Mother America is responsible for her children, responsible, at least to the degree of starting them out upon the race on an equal footing. But the Constitution has ceased to be an important document in one's life, and so one hurries from the analogy.)

The truth is that the black family, in many ways, is ill-equipped to assume the responsibility for the development and growth of the child. The father is so burdened by the daily task of survival that, even were he equipped, his energy is all but dissipated in the struggle for life itself. The mother fares little better. Her life is one crisis after another, the first beginning when she gives birth to her first black child. Yet too, the Negro family is more than likely to be under the influence of the Booker T. Washington philosophy. "There's nothing wrong," Bernice's mother once told us, "with doing a good day's work. I clean Miss A's house, but the Lord don't frown on it 'cause it's honest work."

Honest work it was, and neither of us would argue the contrary. In justifying her own life, however, the old woman was attempting to justify her daughter's life also. There is nothing wrong with being a cleaning woman or a shipyard worker; not every man wants to be a lawyer, a doctor, a teacher, or even a writer. But conversely, not every man wants to be a laborer, and it is here that the Washington philosophy is most pernicious. The assumption is that Blacks are suited only for the most menial of tasks, delegated forever to be the servants and coolies of those who are to build the romantic empire. But more important, such a philosophy removes freedom of choice and substitutes a rigid form of determinism.

"There are more valuable people and less valuable people," remarks the Jewess in Bertolt Brecht's play, *The Private Life of the Master Race:* and we Blacks—dare I say it?—are guilty of using the same categorical division among ourselves that the society at large has used against us. Amos and Bernice were less valuable people because they were poor and black. In the Negro school this was enough to seal their fate. Had they been black and middle class, or light-skinned and poor, this kind of determinism would not have been operative. There would have opened to them an entirely different universe. Their teachers would have felt a sense of responsibility, and taken upon themselves the burden of doing what the family could not do. The boots would have been polished and the straps tightened; somehow a scholarship to college would have been found for them.

"I hope," Amos had confided, "I can get a scholarship." Graduation time came and passed, and although Amos graduated number one and Bernice number two out of a class of sixty-one, no scholarship was forthcoming for either of them. Sometime later, during the summer, one heard rumors that Barbara, whose mother was a teacher, had gotten a scholarship or that Arthur, whose mother was president of the P.T.A. had gotten a scholarship. One never found out whether the rumors were more than just that; but one knows that neither Bernice nor Amos received a scholarship of any sort.

Amos went to work—in the shipyard—to save money to enter Hampton Institute; but the wages paid Negro workers at that time were very little, and by summer's end, what he had been able to save was not enough to even pay for his books for one semester. Yet doggedly, he plowed on, intent on enrolling the next semester; again, the money was not adequate. Semesters came, went, came again, and Amos clung to his dream; but after each semester had passed, the dream became a little less substantial, a little more distant, until soon it had drifted deep into the reservoir of that subconscious where all our unfulfilled dreams eventually end.

Even had they have gone to school, Amos and Bernice may have died mental and spiritual deaths. This we will never know. But they did not go, and somehow the responsibility is not altogether theirs. In a sense, they died because people who should have cared did not; because they were doubly cursed: both black and poor. They died because the people who could have done most to help them were locked like prisoners, within the dungeons of their own egotistical selves.

All of our teachers had problems. They had believed Booker T. Washington, and had, according to their estimates, pulled themselves up by their own bootstraps. They had made themselves valuable to their communities, learned to do something better than anybody else—"learned to do a common thing in an uncommon manner"—and yet they had not solved the problem of color. Perhaps they realized now, the intent of Vardaman's blast against Booker T. Washington, . . . "I am as opposed to Booker T. Washington with all his Anglo-Saxon reinforcements as I am to the . . . typical little 'coon' Andy Dotson, who blacks my shoes every morning."

Here were the Negro teachers, symbolically being linked to the descendants of Andy Dotson, when all their lives they had been trying to get away from Andy Dotson. Where was the justice in a world which could not recognize a man capable of putting distance between himself and his less fortunate fellow man? What could the teachers do to put more mileage between themselves and Andy Dotson? As quickly as possible they had moved away from the Andy Dotsons of the ghettoes; they had forbidden their children to play with the Andy Dotsons of the world; objected when their daughters dated one; protested when one sought to identify with them; joined the white citizens in outrage when one of those Andy Dotsons rioted and destroyed the property of their country; cheered when the criminal Andy Dotson was finally caught in the act of pillage; what more could they do?

"I used to go to the old cowboy and Indian movies," wrote James Baldwin, "and I would always applaud the cowboys until I found out that the Indians were me." Why couldn't our teachers realize that for all their Anglo-Saxon reinforcements, the Andy Dotsons of the world were them?

This is an unfair question, in that it should not be put to the teachers alone. Most of us have tried to kill the Andy Dotson in ourselves in order to prove to the world that we are a separate species. But the ruse has not worked. The cowboy, to paraphrase a French nihilist, draws his six shooter, and fires madly into the crowd at random, and each of us dies an Andy Dotson.

Unable to move beyond their personal sickness, these teachers acquiesced in the death of two young people who did not have to die. It is not important to fix responsibility—for we are all responsible—but we must realize that these young people did not have to die. Until we realize that many more worthy than we have perished in the struggle through no fault of their own, the phrase "I endured" becomes nothing more than the final curtain of a tragedy, where all the actors lie upon the same stage, gored and bleeding to death.

3

WHITE EXPERTS—

BLACK SUBJECTS

THE FIRST EXPERT ON Negro life was the plantation owner who had to evaluate his subject for pragmatic reasons. Viewing the Negro slave on the public auction block, the owner inspected his merchandise closely, feeling a plump limb here, probing for a broken one there, always cognizant that upon his expertise rode hundreds, sometimes thousands of dollars. Later the plantation owner made further evaluations: which of his slaves would make the best house hands, which the best field hands?, which would require, to quote Frederick Douglass, "the most breaking" (the process of beating recalcitrant slaves into submission), which male should mate with which female to produce the best stock; and finally, how much food and clothing would be necessary to sustain the slave during a long day in the fields?

Together with his colleagues, in group meetings or similar gatherings, the owner participated in seminars on the Negro in which each owner contributed the facts revealed through his own scientific investigations. The subject himself took no part in these seminars. He had had little to say, thus far, concerning the voluminous amount of information supposedly held by other people concerning him. His job was merely to prove the experts correct: to be a good field hand or house hand as designated; to provide healthy offspring; to subsist on his allotted rations; and once broken, to remain broken.

To prove the experts correct, however, was often impossible. Frederick Douglass and Nat Turner, to name but two, did not long remain broken. Some field hands were ill-equipped for their assigned tasks, as were some house hands. And the attempt at genetic experimentation ended, often enough, in the kind of failure depicted by Saunders Redding in *No Day of Triumph:* "They kept us locked up in at ol cabin three nights." Julie Lively, a former slave confessed to Redding: "In the morning they let me out an I done my work roun the house, but for three nights ol Doctor Smith lock me up with Baily . . . [But] I didn't have no baby under Baily."

Such failures, however, did not shake the confidence of the experts. As slavery became a national issue, experts on the Negro increased in number, gathering into their ranks politicians, ministers, intellectuals, and scholars.

The most famous of these was Harriet Beecher Stowe, whose novel, *Uncle Tom's Cabin,* became an immediate best seller. The Martin Luther King of her day, Mrs. Stowe set out to awaken the conscience of the nation to the evils of slavery and, in so doing, she created a character whose stereotype survives in the minds of Blacks and whites to the present day. Mrs. Stowe writes of Tom: "He was an expert and efficient workman in whatever he undertook; and was both from habit and principle, prompt and faithful. Quiet and peaceable in his disposition, he hoped, by unremitting diligence, to avert from himself at least a portion of the evils of his conditions."

Tom, then, is good personified, and Mrs. Stowe constructs her novel around the good-evil conflict by depicting the pious, loving black slave in symbolism so angelic that no such character could have existed upon earth. That Mrs. Stowe was able to palm such a fantasy off on her generation was remarkable in light of many contradictory examples presented by Negro slaves themselves. There was little of Tom's piety or love in Nat Turner, Denmark Vessey, Harriet Tubman, or Frederick Douglass.

Laudable though Mrs. Stowe's motives may have been, her portrait of the Negro was no more authentic than that of the plantation owners. She created the Negro not as he was, but as she wished him to be. Having no knowledge of what it meant to be either a slave or a Negro, Mrs. Stowe relied upon her creative imagination to probe dimensions beyond her depth. Like her present day descendants, she viewed her black subjects with the expertise of her own white experience and produced not real people, but grotesque stereotypes, bestowing upon them her ideals, ethics, and values.

Present day experts on the Negro differ from Mrs. Stowe only in methodology. Armed with the tools of research, financed by large foundations, and often a member of Negro organizations, the contemporary Mrs. Stowe pretends to study the subject from an objective vantage point. No objective analysis of the Negro, however, can suffice. A present day Joseph K., the Afro-American lives in the center of that dark, mysterious abyss peopled by fantasies and illusions, where he is confronted by frustration and plagued by demons of persecution; and only those who are capable of plunging into the abyss, of living in that hell of anguish and despair; only those who are capable of dredging from the dank interiors of their own wretched souls a vision of the human spirit in agony can see the black soul, stretched across the torture rack of history, in all of its power, beauty, and despair.

This is to say that most whites are incapable of portraying Blacks with any degree of reality. "The Negro," writes Saunders Redding in *On Being Negro in America*, "lives constantly on two planes of awareness"; and Redding's statement has its antecedent in W.E.B. DuBois' classic analysis of the Negro psyche in *Souls of Black Folk:* "One ever feels his twoness; an American, a Negro; two souls, two thoughts, two unreconciled strivings; two warring ideals in one dark body, whose dogged strength alone keeps it from being torn asunder."

Like slavery, such a dimension constitutes a barrier beyond which the white mind cannot peer. The complexities of being black in American Society are so varied that few Negroes are capable of interpreting them; and the day by day experiences of the average Black in America are such as to belie belief. These are unique experiences, and the Negro's reactions to them are unique reactions, owing little to white idealism, morality, or ethics. "This society," James Baldwin wrote to his nephew, "set you down in the ghetto to die"; and all Negroes have been enclosed in some such ghetto. To scale its walls, requires the kind of experience peculiar only to the ghettoized.

Negroes, at long last, are beginning to realize this fact. Lawrence P. Neal in an essay, "White Liberals vs. Black Community," in the July, 1966 issue of *Liberator* magazine, writes: "Presently, the dissemination and examination of the main features of Afro-American life and culture are not in the hands of black people, but rather, in that of whites." Neal suggests that: "Black intellectuals and artists cannot expect any meaningful development until we assume more power over all aspects of our culture . . ."

No such realization, however, has occurred to whites. In an anthology, *Essays of Our Times*, edited by Leo Hamalian and Edmond Volpe, the essays selected to deal with Negro life were written by two white men: Norman Mailer and John Fischer. "Norman Mailer," write the editors, "has said that the function of a writer is to see life 'as others do not see it.' As the 'White Negro' indicates, he performs this function brilliantly and provocatively . . ." Mailer's motives, like those of Mrs. Stowe, are perhaps laudable, yet his portrait of Negroes is no less fanciful or imaginative, and Mailer in no way demonstrates the ability to see black life as others do not see it.

"Knowing in the cells of his existence that life was war," Mailer reports, "the Negro (all exceptions admitted) could rarely afford the sophisticated inhibitions of civilization, and so he kept for his survival the art of the primitive, subsisted for his Saturday night kicks, relinquishing the pleasures of the mind for the obligatory pleasures of the body . . ." But Mailer's imagination knows no boundaries; and later he sees the Negro "forced into the position of exploring all those moral wildernesses of civilized society . . . and not being privileged to gratify his self-esteem with the heady satisfaction of categorical condemnation [the Negroes] chose to move instead in that other direction . . . in the worst of perversion, promiscuity, pimpery, drug addiction, rape, razor-slash, bottle break, what have you . . ."

One is never insulted by Mailer, only slightly amused. Yet one must question the judgment of scholars who fail to examine the credentials of their experts. Mailer's characterization of Negroes, far from being unique, has its genesis as far back as the first anthropologist. Moreover, the underlying thesis of Mailer's essay differs little from the underlying thesis of Richard Wright's *Native Son*, in which Wright suggests that the resurrection of white America rests upon the resurrection of America's Bigger Thomases who are relegated to the bottom of the societal heap. In the same way Mailer sees the Negro as the Christ-figure, resurrecting America by transforming her into the Negro's image.

Wright, however, living continually in that world of pessimism spurred by hatred, fear, anger, and bitterness which is a part of every Black's experience, could not possibly, entertain such abstract ideals for long. Mailer, on the other hand, securely ensconsed behind a white barricade, can continue to look at the Negro through eyes tinged with optimism.

If the choice of the "White Negro" by Mailer evidences an error in selection, the choice of John Fischer's "What the Negro Needs Most: A First Class Citizen's Council", represents a serious error in judgment. Whereas Mailer amuses, Fischer insults, not by his statements but by the posture of moral physician to the Negro people which he assumes.

"So long," says Fischer, "as the Negro blames his plight entirely on circumstances, history, and the white man, he is going to stay in that plight. He will get out of it only when he begins to change his circumstances, make new history, and shoulder a bigger share of responsibility for the fix he is in." (One is reminded of the story of the lynch mob, enjoying its beer and hot dogs, as the body of a Negro swung in the breeze. "You think God will blame us for this?" asked one of the members. "Hell no!" replied another, "God knows it's that nigger's fault for lettin' himself be lynched.")

Yet Fischer's prognostication is worse than his diagnosis. According to him, what the Negro needs in order to become a respected member of the American society is "a First Class Citizen's Council. Its purpose [will be] the genuine integration of Negroes into the normal streams of American life." A stream is like a looking glass. One looks at the images reflected and determines in his own mind whether they are true or distorted. Despite occasional ripples in "the normal stream of American life," Fischer concludes that the overall image reflected is that of an integrated society. Because the image is true for him, he assumes that it is true for most men. Such an assumption, fathered by arrogance, must be vigorously contested.

To many Negroes, the "normal stream of American life" is a stream polluted beyond purification. It is a stream reeking with hatred and bigotry, and festering with racism. The waters of the stream have been muddied by one hundred years of lynching, brutalization, persecution, and every form of degradation which man has been capable of imposing upon his fellow man. The stream flows from North to South, East to West, and its waters are the same on each shore. That the Negro desires to cleanse himself in such a stream could only be suggested by one who has little knowledge of the complex psyche of an American Negro.

"We have been believers," says Margaret Walker. But today, the belief in an America freed of racism, fear, and hate is a belief which few Blacks have either the time or interest to indulge in. Instead, Negroes, are more likely to be asking with the late Lorraine Hansberry, "Who wants to integrate into a burning house?" But, specifically, the black intellectual is more apt to be engaged in the serious task of reappraising the values administered to him by such physicians as John Fischer.

The result can only be a repudiation of such values. Looking into the black psyche, exploring the souls of his own people, and recognizing the distorted images propounded by experts from the plantation owners to the twentieth century physicians, the Afro-American has begun to piece together out of his own experiences, "a new table of the laws"; and, in so doing, he has begun to recognize the great disparity between his aspirations and those attributed to him by others.

That such a reevaluation is taking place in the black ghettoes of this country will come as a shock to many white experts who will recoil from the fact that the subject no longer looks at America through the rose tinted glasses of his ancestors. Even more will fail to understand why Franz Fanon's *The Wretched of the Earth* has become a best seller among black intellectuals; and none will wish to believe that, the opinion polls to the contrary, the most powerful idea in the black ghetto today is the idea of Black Power.

For what Black Power means for many Negroes is a repudiation of the values, morals, and ethics of a white majority. Black Power means an exploration of black culture; and the realization that within this culture are those values which a black minority can, without shame, embrace. Black Power means the coming together of men as brothers, in a way far beyond white America's ability to comprehend.

More significantly however, Black Power is a creative concept aimed at destroying one hundred years of mental enslavement, distorted images, and meaningless clichés. As such, Black Power is a rebuke to white experts who do not realize that to be black in America is to journey through the fiery, labyrinthine corridors of hell; and only those who are capable of embarking upon such a journey can fulfill the first requisite for competent scholarship: to know one's subject intimately and well.

4

LETTER TO A

WHITE COLLEAGUE

DEAR LENNIE,

I have decided to answer your private letter in a public manner. I will attempt to do so without betraying the more personal
aspects of your correspondence. My decision is dictated by my
intention to clear the air—which has become excessively polluted
over the past year—between myself and my friends, both black
and white. I find that their central questions are the same as those
that you have put to me so eloquently in your letter; therefore in
answering you, I shall also be answering them.

I said that this is a public correspondence which does not mean
in any sense that it is not personal. Indeed, it is personal in the
most important sense, that is to say, it is personal to me. The statements I make here are binding upon no other black man in this
country, for, to paraphrase Saunders Redding, I have never been
enclothed with the authority to speak for others. Therefore, the
truth which I record here is personal and may or may not find
accord in the hearts and minds of the millions of black people
across this country.

I am very adamant on this subject. I remember all too well my
own bitter and violent reactions to those who, over the years,
have pretended to speak for me. I was incensed, I suppose, partly
at the egotistical assumption of that being who attempts to speak
for twenty million other beings; but more so, I was incensed be-

43

cause society, in listening to such egoists, was communicating with me by proxy which is the most effective way of denying my humanity.

I know that society could not deal with twenty million of us individually. However, it could have dealt with us long ago (as it must deal with us now—as men of differing temperaments, persuasions, and ideologies in those areas so fundamental to our destiny), and listened, not to the solitary voices of specially bred and selected nightingales, but to the many voices of discord among us—those which dared to articulate truths profoundly believed by many of us. Such voices are not comforting to hear. They speak of turmoil, strife, and war, and herald the possible coming of racial warfare; none of which is designed to placate or comfort white America.

But Americans desire comfort above all else, and it is indeed more comforting to listen to Booker T. Washington, A. Philip Randolph, and Roy Wilkins than W.E.B. DuBois, Marcus Garvey, and Malcolm X. And today, it is far more comforting to listen to the responsible Negro leaders than to those leaderless millions who voice their grievances in actions and terminology so different from that of their purported leaders.

It is this, I suppose, which causes me to be pessimistic. In the wake of the riots of the previous summers, society still does business with the old combine which has returned nothing but empty dividends to its stockholders. Each Molotov cocktail thrown in the ghetto, each store looted, each sniper's bullet expended, negates the assertions of Negro leaders, and reveals their influence to be bankrupt and impotent for all, save those who insist that Armageddon can be staved off forever by accepting myths and half truths which offer the promise of temporary comfort.

This is the best way of approaching your question regarding the importance of Black Power. Because white people have preferred to deal with only certain members of the black community, a serious effort at dialogue among black people was averted. This was accomplished in the most insidious manner. That individual who more nearly articulated the grievances of the Negro Upper and Middle Classes, and who was, in turn, willing to accept the dictates of the white power establishment, became the liaison between the black and white communities. With this position went power, prestige, and money.

Such men, as Booker T. Washington proved, were remarkably capable of using that power—more often than not to stifle dissent. Washington, for example, marshalled, often by cajolery and threats, the support of every Negro newspaper in America with the exception of one, in his debate with W.E.B. DuBois; and only DuBois' strength and determination enabled him to carry on a struggle against such power.

Again, Malcolm X, who sought to produce among Blacks a dialogue centered around those affairs which concerned black people, was vilified in the press, both black and white. In both instances such actions were possible only because the Negro leaders had the unqualified support of the white liberal establishment which knew only one thing about the projected dialogue—that it would not be very comforting to white people.

What, you might ask, does this have to do with Black Power? For those of us who have demanded a debate between the ideological opponents in the Black community—Integrationist versus Nationalist—Stokely Carmichael's injection of the phrase "Black Power" into the civil rights struggle was the most important accomplishment in the history of this ideological war in the last one hundred years.

I am, to be sure, a Nationalist, and there has never been a day in my life during which I did not want Black Power. I did not call it by that name and I had no formula by which it could be attained; yet I thought seriously about it and I seriously desired it. At the age of six, when I read articles and saw pictures of a black man who had been lynched in Mississippi, I wanted Black Power. Twenty years later, when I was slapped by a racist policeman in New York City, I wanted Black Power. And even when in college, confronting a professor who openly professed his bigotry, I wanted Black Power. In other words, I wanted some way of controlling my own life; but most of all, I wanted some way of controlling those who had control of my life.

I was not alone. Many young people thought as I did. Yet we had no forum and we had no power. Society dictated what it wanted to hear and appointed those whom it wished to hear. We, made impotent, carried on debates among ourselves, always in small numbers, knowing that the thoughts which other men attributed to us were false; but knowing too, that we were powerless to expose the fallacy. The things which we say now with impunity, we did not say then, not entirely out of fear, but more out of a sense of futility. We were the young Davids, and the Goliaths were far too powerful.

What were the things we said? We uttered the same "Get Whitey!", and "Hate Whitey!" epithets which you so deplore today. Make no mistake about it; "Get Whitey!" is not a new phrase, not the exclusive property of poor and uneducated Negroes. Few of us in this country have not voiced such an epithet, and fewer still have not meant it. For my part, I do not apologize. This is a stage through which I had to go. To bypass it would have meant to deny a fundamental part of my experiences in this country and to be less than honest with myself. I could not realize that my hating Whitey was unimportant to my functioning as a man until I had admitted that I hated him.

Today more of us are admitting this fact and perhaps here, if anywhere, lies our salvation. Once this step is passed, we can then proceed to the central issue confronting us as Black People—serious debate as to what our collective goals are. We will no longer allow men who hold monologues only with themselves to decide for us the most important goals of our lives. This has been the situation since the close of the Martin Delaney-Frederick Douglass debates one hundred years ago. Since that time Black people have been unable to carry on a debate among themselves; partly because white power would not allow it, but also because the time was not appropriate for an alternative to integration to be publicly enunciated and wholeheartedly supported.

The rebellions in the ghettoes of the past summers brought about the appropriate time; and Black Power was born as the other alternative. Never mind that white people do not understand Black Power, never mind that many Negroes oppose it. Certainly it is no panacea, no magic key to Canaan, no paved stairway to paradise; but one thing it is: it is the other alternative to propositions put forward, debated and agreed upon by men who had little rapport with those whom they purported to represent. As such, it is a guarantee that, for some time to come, there will be a serious debate among black people in this country concerning their own aims—one could expect far less from a slogan, no one has a right to expect more.

This leads me to your central question. What part can an individual such as yourself play at the present time? Granted that you are sincere; that your motives are impelled, not by a search for power, nor by a wish to purge yourself of some unknown guilt; that you honestly see in your Jewish experience, correlatives which enable you to equate, to a degree, some aspects of that experience with mine.

Let me be very blunt. Your role must be minimal. You may continue to teach black students, to write about those conditions which produce poverty, crime, and rebellion, to work in any area or organization dedicated to the alleviation of those ills which we both deplore. Beyond this, however, you cannot go. In the dialogue between black man and black man, none of your credentials —neither your sincerity nor your humanitarian interests—qualify you for participation. I will be even more candid! The necessary qualification for participation in such a dialogue is a black skin.

Many of us are convinced that the present debate will at long last clarify the goals of black people in this country—not just for a few, but for many. It is incumbent, then, upon every black person, no matter his ideological persuasion, to take an active part in the debate. But the debate is a private, personal, family affair. A husband and wife, so to speak, are attempting to work out their relationship vis-à-vis the outside world; and only the husband and wife can determine what that relationship will be.

This should come as no surprise to you. It was Moses, a Jew, who had to lead the Israelites out of Egypt. The job could not have been entrusted to an Egyptian, no matter the degree of his sincerity. It is Catholics who must choose a new Pope, make dogma, pass on ideology, and formulate principles for the Catholic Church. No outsider can perform this function, for no outsider can have that information, varied as it must be, which will allow him to comment intelligently on issues important to the future of the church. Indeed, the counsel of an outsider may be more disruptive than constructive.

Such is the position of the present debate in this country. It is one which, in the last analysis, only black people can resolve. White people, no matter how sincere, must remain outside as mere, interested observers. This is as true of white people who support Black Power as it is of those who oppose it. We demand the right to choose for ourselves the paths we wish to follow; whether integration or segregation, peace and tranquility or continued hostility and war, whether mutual cooperation or separate, individual endeavor; but most important, we reserve the right to choose those who will represent us, who will be emissaries from us to you.

Carmichael is correct. There will come a time in our history when a dialogue between whites and Blacks is possible. But that time can come only when we ourselves have "taken care of business"; that is, transformed our inner dialogue into a realistic monologue, decided upon our goals, and are ready to present America with a list of demands which all of us accept in the main, if not specifically.

Should we not have such an exclusive dialogue? It would seem to me that only men of narrow vision would attempt to prevent it. Yet, such men there are. One reads daily, in the white and black press, vilifications of Black Power proponents and gross distortions of their ideas. We are constantly informed that "Black Power is disruptive," that it is separatism, that, in the words of one Negro leader, "it is an invitation to suicide." This may well be. Yet who can decide for another people, even in the case of suicide, whether or not the act is desirable? Only the people themselves can decide, and they can decide only when men of differing ideas are willing to submit those ideas to be debated, agreed upon or rejected.

Let us suppose, for example, that the "Responsible Negro Leaders" who continue to see integration as the goal for twenty million people do not have faulty vision. Let us suppose that they are correct when they argue that the majority of Blacks in this country support their "moderate leadership." What, then, should these leaders do? They should be willing to subject their ideas to the supreme test; that is, take their postulations to the black churches, lodge halls, colleges, and ghettos of this country, and have their positions authenticated by the only ones capable of honestly doing so, black people themselves.

This has not happened. Negro leaders prefer to address their appeals to white America, to gain support from such men as you who have no way of determining whether their claims are legitimate or not. Like Booker T. Washington, they exercise their power in the most negative way, attempting to silence those who refuse to accept their truths as gospel.

Some whites have been trapped into supporting them in this endeavor. The N.A.A.C.P. had every right to invite Vice President Humphrey to its annual convention in 1967. Vice President Humphrey had no right to castigate Black Power. In so doing, he infringed on a private debate—one of which he knows very little —and thus lost a chance at statesmanship—the chance to welcome a vigorous, healthy debate among a people seriously concerned with their own destiny.

Do not, my friend, make this mistake. At this stage of race relations, young and inquisitive men are conscientiously seeking a way out of that Götterdämmerung which confronts us. They are by no means homogeneous. There are great differences among them. But only when these young men have seriously debated the issues, can there be any hope that you and I may live in a society where men are respected on the basis of individual worth.

Their task is difficult enough. It must not be made more so by men who are primarily interested in their own comfort. For these young men have arrived at a truth which their elders have not yet been able to grasp—in a society where some men are regarded as less than human, there should be no comfort for anyone. No, not for you, nor for me, and certainly not for those millions of Americans whose concern about the destiny of their country will only be made aware to them when they awaken one morning and are forced to dig themselves out of the rubble of a Detroit or a Newark.

Comfort is a luxury which must be earned, and Americans have not earned the right to be comfortable. Those of us who support Black Power are determined that America will not be until she has earned that right. Perhaps this is a dangerous position for a member of a predominantly white university faculty to take in these troubled times. Yet, so high are the stakes that those of us who have welcomed in the new dialogue are prepared, in the interests of truth, to make any sacrifice. But more important, we are prepared to bring the issues to debate, to bring our ideas before black people and, if they are rejected, we are equally prepared, in the words of the poet, "to accept the verdict and the doom assigned."

Yours,

Addison Gayle, Jr.

5

THE CABINET

OF THE MIND

LATELY, I HAVE SENSED a strange uneasiness on the part of friends
who still retain intellectual and physical contact with me. Some
have read my writings and openly questioned my sanity. Others
have spent long hours debating with me, attempting to convince
me that I am a fraud, that I do not harbor the anxieties and hates
which, in their opinion, make me a twentieth century monster.
One suggested, quite seriously, that I leave the country.

These friends, Black and white, view me, as a special kind of
subversive agent, no challenge to them physically but an undeniable affront to their positions as intellectual prophets. Conceiving
of Afro-Americans as things, these people have constructed special cabinets of the mind in which we, like fragile glassware, are
assigned specific positions. One's position is dependent upon his
success—or purported success, which means the same thing—in
the American society. Having attained some measure of success, a
higher shelf in that special cabinet of the mind has been reserved
for me than, for example, some of my best friends in the ghetto.

I am an expensive piece of glassware, not because of my present success—professors are a dime a bushel—but, I am told, because
of my promise, and my youth which makes it probable that my
promise will be fulfilled. My only task, I am constantly reminded,
is to rip away that aberration, that incestuous cancer, that de-
monic something within me which makes me fill the ears of my

listeners with curses, the hearts of my wellwishers with despair and the minds of my sympathizers with anger and scorn. Still, I am an expensive piece of glassware, an object of value used only for the best courses—those dished out by negro leaders and the society pages of negro magazines. In all such propagandistic feasts I am exhibited—cautioned to be moderate, at least for now— praised for my unscarred countenance, marvelled at for my sheen and polish ("you speak very well," remarked a lifelong liberal) and hailed for my endurance.

Lately, however, I have become restive, begun to fidget on the shelf, unable to remain moderate, and begun to suggest that my special niche is one of which I am undeserving, that I belong on the bottom rung with the scarred, cracked, dust-colored glass-ware. At this point my friends start to drift away. For their "cen-ter," as Yeats says, "cannot hold." The demon within me cannot be exorcised, not by any medicine which they have so far pro-duced; and this demon existing in me, threatening to erupt, is enough to bring chaos if not destruction to their mythological cosmic apparatus.

They have been the victims of myths. They have hypnotized themselves into believing myths not of their own concoction and certainly not of mine. Beset by stereotypes foisted upon them by the white world, like the early Black writers, they have attempted to destroy the stereotypes, not through reason and logic but, in-stead, by offering stereotypes of their own, usually more gro-tesque and imaginary than the ones they were designed to replace.

Denouncing Harriet Beecher Stowe's Uncle Tom as unrealis-tic and insulting, my friends have turned to the pages of Booker T. Washington's autobiography, echoing Washington in asserting that: "No white American ever thinks that any other race is wholly civilized until he wears the white man's clothes, eats the white man's food, speaks the white man's language, and professes the white man's religion." The New Negro, therefore, is no Uncle Tom, no cowering, pitying, tenderhearted old slave, "quiet and peaceable in his disposition, hoping by unremitting diligence to avert from himself at least a portion of the evils of his condi-tion."

Instead, this New Negro is obsessed with his own peculiar

manifest destiny, as prescribed by Washington during one of those interminable excursions into the backwaters of the South to bestow a benevolent smile upon the "culturally deprived masses": "The work to be done in order to lift these people up seemed almost beyond accomplishing—I wondered if I could accomplish anything, and if it were worthwhile for me to try."

Now begins the philosophy of the cabinet of the mind: the process of categorizing people as though they were pieces of china—a process begun in slavery where, like objects, Black men were shelved in terms of house niggers and field niggers, good niggers and bad niggers; objects usable either in the master's house or in the fields. The New Negro, however, like Washington, is capable of divining his own worth, of evaluating himself and thereby setting himself off from other Afros, thus refining that process begun by the white master. More sophisticated than Uncle Tom and more fearful of black Simon Legrees than white ones, the New Negro has dedicated himself to mapping out a blueprint by which he and his white friends may live in peace and harmony. Though the stance is new, the old voice of the "great educator" echoes like a ventriloquist from their mouths: "—any individual who (learns) to do something better than anybody else —(learns) to do a common thing in an uncommon manner— (has) solved his problem regardless of the colour of his skin, and in proportion as the Negro (learns) to produce what other people (want) and must have, in the same proportion (will) he be respected."

The salient feature of the new stereotype was respect. Uncle Tom was pitied, mostly by white people who knew too little of Afro-Americans to discern fact from fiction, but what the New Negro demanded was respect, albeit a respect predicated upon the belief that in that vast world of inequality there were, still, some Black men who were more equal than others; and that these few could be granted their due recognition by appeals to a mythological American conscience. Washington's statement was written for white men and delivered before white men whom Washington took to be representative of the American conscience. And it was these white men who chose Booker T. Washington as a negro leader, thus elevating him above other Negroes and making him the personification of the New Negro, the living exemplar of the new stereotype.

The New Negro occupied the top shelf in that cabinet of the mind. He became the man with whom to do business, the man to control the Black militants—those insane men within the race who believed that the American conscience was more oriented towards the philosophy of the Ku Klux Klan than that of Jesus Christ. As a result, there came into being a combination of white and negro leaders joined together by a pernicious contract which segregated Negroes within the race, forcing the dissidents underground, stifling debate, and destroying the Afro-American's initiative to assert himself individually.

In a Southern town, not atypical, my father and a small group of radicals confronted this combined white and negro power in the summer of 1938. In the local shipyard, the sole reservoir for Black labor, Black workers were subjected to every conceivable form of indignity. They were forced to drink from segregated water fountains, to use dirty segregated latrines, to stand in segregated waiting lines for lunch; they were given the dirtiest jobs, fired more frequently, and hired at lower wages than whites of lesser schooling or experience.

This was possible because the shipyard had its own bargaining union which was more representative of the interests of management than of workers, Black or white. A mulatto was the liaison between the Black workers and the white management, though a white liaison official had as much power, or more, over the fate of Black workers as the mulatto official. In fact, negroes often admitted that they would rather take their grievances to the white official from whom they could gain a measure of sympathy, not forthcoming from the mulatto.

Together with an outside force, my father sought to have a national union, which would be more representative of the workers, substituted for the old management-dominated union then in existence. Black laborers, though not a majority, constituted a large percentage of those eligible to vote; if they were to combine with those whites who were aware of the advantages of an outside arbitrating body, the election could be won. To this end, rallies were held throughout the city, and many on both sides of the issue believed that the days of the old shipyard union were numbered.

None however, and especially the opponents of the old union, had accurately gauged the power—nor the determination to use that power—of the white and negro leaders in the city. In a post-election letter, written to a friend in New York, my father explained: "Negroes, most of whom I had known all my life came to me, in shame, telling me that they knew we were right, but R—(the negro banker) threatened to foreclose mortgages if the new union won, and to evict from those pigpens of homes around Warwick Avenue those who voted against the old union. Ministers denounced the new union from the pulpit—some seeming to discover for the first time that I am a Communist and labeling the new union Communist also—as troublemaking and anti-Christ. I would bet my life that the telephone lines between B—(the white dentist, Mayor of the city) and W—(a negro leader) were on fire. We can do little here until we destroy this damn alliance."

Despite the costs to the masses—and the costs were great indeed—such alliances helped disseminate the stereotype of the New Negro. Whites were enamored of the patient, reasonable, rational negro who realized that his fate was bound inextricably to that of whites and that furthermore some measure of recognition, of status, was available to those who adopted the Protestant Ethic, who struggled to disengage themselves from the uncivilized, culturally deprived masses. True to the Washington philosophy, such men pulled themselves up by their own bootstraps, showed what could be accomplished in America despite the racial band, displayed the frontier spirit, and emerged from the jungle of the past as living testaments to the future.

Such negroes, victims of their own egotism, saw themselves in the role of Franklin Frazier's stereotype: descendants of those who "had been enslaved, and had suffered many disabilities since emancipation, (yet who) on the whole were well off economically, had gained civil rights, and had improved their status. Therefore what had happened to them during slavery, which was after all a mild paternalistic system, should be forgotten along with the other injustices which they have suffered since. More-over, their economic position was superior to that of other peo-ples of the world, especially the colored peoples."

The significance of such a portrait of the Afro-American es-capes no one. For in the first place, such portraits perpetuate the division between the house niggers and the field niggers, between the Black blessed and the Black damned, and construct status hierarchies by which men, robbed of human dignity, can find some modicum of security, retain some semblance of respect for their own worth as men, can sit securely upon some mountain top and peer down condescendingly upon their less fortunate fellows. Moreover, like all stereotypes, this new evaluation of the Black man serves to deny the realistic portraitures of the past, to erase from the minds of white and Black alike the reality of the exist-ence of such men as Denmark Vesey, Nat Turner, Frederick Douglass, and David Walker. Such men become the invisible men of American history, far removed from the consciousness of the New Negro, existing, if at all, in the minds of a few Afro-Americans who feel more akin to them than to the new prophets.

Yet Vesey, Turner, Douglass, and Walker were revolutionar-ies—and in that cabinet of the mind which the New Negro has constructed there are no shelves for such men. Like white men, Black men also are suspicious of revolutionaries, those whose act-ions constantly challenge a philosophy of passivity and patience. Martin Luther King reached far more negroes than Malcolm X, not because King's philosophy is sounder—safer maybe, but not sounder—but because King appealed to the dominant desire of the majority of negroes to be good niggers as opposed to bad niggers, conformists as opposed to individuals, bourgeois as opposed to proletariat. "Negroes," some negro leader (probably Wilkins or Young) has remarked, "are conservative on everything but the race issue." This is an understatement. The majority of them, even those in the Watts' and Harlems of America, are racial con-servatives as well, aspiring more to become middle-class misfits than healthy, human beings.

The exploits of the Black revolutionaries of the past have been expunged from the minds of the majority of America's Black population. And it is this which makes my protestations suspect, my thoughts treacherous and my opinions dangerous. For men possessing no knowledge of Nat Turner cannot begin, even in an infantile way, to understand me. Men enamored of the new stereotype who have lived so long in a hypocritical world peopled by Booker T. Washingtons are incapable of interpreting my world peopled by the ghosts of neurotic, troubled, desperate Nat Turners. Further, men unable to find meaning, hope and life in the futile, perhaps naive, yet brutal rebellion of Nat Turner which was initiated in an orgy of blood and culminated in death by lynching—such men cannot possibly understand the meaning which the riots in California, Chicago and New York hold for me.

Yet the riots do hold meanings, profound ones. They attest to the fact that a new generation of Afro-Americans is uncomfortable with the new stereotypes, unwilling to be considered little more than fragile glassware placed at random into cabinets constructed by the naive, fanciful minds of people who have no cognizance of human worth, no respect for human dignity, and utter contempt for the human spirit. Each Black soul in the ghetto who shouts out in a paranoiac frenzy of looting and rioting is shouting to a group of monsters who would categorize his humanity by transforming it into an object that the human spirit is never so depleted of hope, vigor and anger that it cannot muster the strength for rebellion, even if—and all of us know this—rebellion must end in defeat, in mass murder by those who possess America's most important attribute—power.

Surely Nat Turner realized this fact. One could not exist in the era of slavery without realizing certain fundamental facts about one's existence: how much the continuation of existence depended upon the whims and fancies of one's master; how great, awesome and all-encompassing was the power of the master; how completely stifled, shut-in and hopeless one's own life was relative to ambition, growth and freedom of thought and movement.

Is it any wonder, then, that, like Sojourner Truth and Harriet Tubman, Nat Turner would hear voices and see visions urging him to undertake the liberation of his people? On August 21, 1831, Turner obeyed the dictates of these subconscious utterances and began the revolt which has now been all but wiped away from the pages of American history. The first to fall were those closest to the rebellion, the members of the family of Turner's master, John Travis. In addition, some sixty whites were killed before the rioters and their leader were hanged for the insurrection.

Too little has been written about the followers of Nat Turner. Seventy slaves joined the revolt; seventy men, not unmindful of the consequences, dedicated themselves to a hopeless, futile rebellion, engaged in an act of suicide and chose to gain freedom in the only way that freedom can be gained with honor—by wrenching it from the hands of the master through violence. There must have been those, nevertheless, who argued the pragmatic realities of the case: seventy men comprised a minuscule force in comparison to the majority number of whites; all the means of waging warfare were in the hands of whites—all power, all recourse to weapons, everything necessary to stop a rebellion; furthermore, given the tyrannical nature of the master in times of peace, what would that nature be in times of insurrection?

Each of the seventy knew the answer to such a question. Yet these men had heard voices and seen visions; and though to all rational men the utterances of the voices and the images projected by the visions were insane, to men for whom the rational and the irrational are one and the same, sanity and insanity are irrelevant terms. The voices and the visions were only secondary factors, wish fulfillments perhaps, of men who, though knowing, despaired of admitting the futility of their purported acts. For long before the sound of the first imagined voice, they had decided, in the chaotic jungle of horror and discontent where the Black soul nestles, that what existed was the worst, and that therefore nothing, not even death, could bring about a condition more terrible than that in which they daily lived.

Yet the New Negro, the maker of cabinets, sees no parallel between Turner's rebellion and the rebellions in the Black ghettos of present-day America. Such men are fenced in by their own constructions, forced to think in terms of criteria set up by their own minds, dedicated to distorting those truths which jeopardize their security, peace and comfort. They have acquiesced in the annihilation of the image of Nat Turner and his followers in an attempt to keep alive that stereotype which allows their narrow worlds to stave off destruction—a stereotype that omits the ominous truth that in American society today there exist hundreds of thousands of Nat Turners for whom no peace can be had, no calm can come, no sustenance found except in the final flaming Armageddon of violence and destruction predicted by the biblical prophets.

To these men the revolutionaries in America's ghettos are insane. And, certainly, according to the reality of the position of Black men in America—a condition analogous to that of Turner and his followers during slavery—violent rebellion is suicidal, self-destructive, and fruitless. James Weldon Johnson summed up the situation in 1928: "We would be justified in taking up arms or anything we could lay our hands on and fighting for the common rights we are entitled to and denied, if we had a chance to win. But I know and we all know there is not a chance."

Johnson's prophecy is one for rational men capable of remaining so in a society which exists on the irrational principle that some men are more human than others. And though in his private heart each Black man agrees with Johnson, still, to that scarred, bruised, desperate soul come voices and visions negating rationality and propelling him to suicidal undertakings. Almost to the man, the rioters in Watts, in Harlem, in Bedford Stuyvesant knew that rebellion would end in injury, death, or jail. No one who concocted a Molotov cocktail was unaware that to throw it meant to bring down annihilation upon him. Yet men made Molotov cocktails, and men faced tanks and guns, taking the existential leap into manhood by defying reason, logic, and history. "The lion is alone, and so am I," shouted Byron's Manfred. And each rioter, likewise, was aware of his alienation even from those closest to him. For most Afro-Americans the journey to manhood is a lonely, solitary expedition over frightful, fear-laden passages of the spirit and soul. More Joseph K than Bigger Thomas, the Black American has even been deprived of the luxury of accidentally falling into manhood, of bribing his way in with the currency of historical pride. Each step has been painful, grueling, and torturous; and for only a few has the goal been reached.

Some, like the rioters, would know freedom and thus manhood for one short moment, for the brief span of time between the rioting night and the daylight calm. There in the darkness broken only by the flares of red, revolving lights from police vehicles and the flaming, meteor-like tail of smoke of the Molotov cocktail, in the still, hushed night interrupted by screams of terror, of curses, of jubilation, some few Black men who had never before known freedom and who after tonight would, perhaps, never know freedom again were enraptured by a maddening, panoramic frenzy bordering upon mania. After long years of interment the ghost of Nat Turner was revived, and men, drunk with frustration, fought their way into that dream state of freedom so peculiar to the dispossessed of the earth.

Others, however, being trapped by their own psychology, will never know freedom. Like most Americans the New Negro has misinterpreted the *Zeitgeist* of the twentieth century. Being accustomed to categorizing people as things, the cabinetmakers have built categories and erected criteria by which men and women may be sorted and shuffled away into obscure niches oblivious to history.

These categories label certain Afro-Americans, rob those in the ghetto of visibility, depict those on the bottom shelves of the cabinets as things without substance, without feeling, without a claim upon normal life. Others in American society, moving from this philosophical base into abstraction, view this "thing" as dangerous—in which case one starves it, abuses it mentally in a million different ways and, when in doubt, lynches it—or as loving, in which case one reveres it, looks upon it with paternal amusement, elevates it to the status of a redeemer: the Christ figure who will resurrect fallen America.

Few see the Black man as representative of modern man in the twentieth century, beset with all those problems which confront twentieth century man. The Afro-American is more alienated than Dostoyevsky's underground man because he has known loneliness for a much longer period of time; he is more terrified than Kafka's Joseph K because for a much longer time he has been the victim of forces beyond his control; he is more capable of murder than Richard Wright's Bigger Thomas because today the channels through which manhood is attained are more closed.

Each Black American, then, alone with his private soul, is closeted with a murderer, and no amount of distortion can erase this fact. The mania of twentieth century man is rebellion; and for the Afro-American, rebellion can only end in murder—his own or his oppressors'. Yet those given to sentimentality, those who catalogue the Afro-American in terms of love, meekness, and passivity, those makers of cabinets who would divide a race into categories, will vehemently dispute this argument. They will unpack the old clichés, drag out the old shibboleths, argue that "Negroes are people like everybody else"; "the Negro loves America"; "violence is futile"; "Negroes are not violent by nature"; "the Negro knows that he can only win his freedom in cooperation with well-meaning whites."

Such apologists should, however, closet themselves alone—as I have done—with their thoughts and, reinforcing those thoughts, the experiences of living in a society where every hour is one of torment, every day one of frustration, every waking moment beset with real and imagined horrors. Let each of them awaken, sometimes, as I have, in the middle of the night, and scream out to some nameless God to destroy his enemies, or to take that life which to him is meaningless, yet to which he clings so fervently.

Let the apologists confront themselves, own up to their Blackness and realize that the long years of chasing the stereotype, of attempting to appease an American conscience by deceit and by sacrificing freedom of emotion, of despair, of the thought of revenge, have resulted in an America grown sanguine, perhaps guilt-ridden, but nevertheless callous and unrepentant, towards its oppressed on the bottom shelf of those many cabinets of the mind.

The Afro-American is a tormented being, and these cabinet makers—especially the negro carpenter—must realize this fact. A special shelf must be constructed to house a kind of chinaware no longer peculiar to America but representative of all the earths dispossessed. The New Afro is to be found, therefore, not in Booker T. Washington's *Autobiography*, but instead in Franz Fanon's *The Wretched Of The Earth;* and the character in these pages is to be found in the Black ghettos of America, where amidst the symbols of decay and death, the people themselves are the most vigorous, most dynamic exemplars of life. For such people are assured that what exists at present is the worst; the conditions of life under which they and their children now live have no parallels anywhere else in American society. Is it any wonder, then, that such men will set forward upon an adventure which can bring surcease to a tormented mind only through an orgy of violence and destruction?

When I make such statements, it frightens my friends, and causes them to hold me in disrepute, to question my sanity. They admit that they have taken no such excursions into themselves, as I suggest, never laid themselves open before the mirror of their own minds, never attempted to explicate their inner thoughts. In short, like most Americans they are aware of only one truth and desire neither to hear nor to believe in another.

My truth, they argue, will not make them free but, on the contrary, ensnare them more, cause the societal vise to tighten, close the few doors now open to them, reinforce the theories of white racists, and drive away their many sincere, white friends. Perhaps, they concede, they do exist in a half-hypocritical, half-deceptive world; yet the norm of their society is hypocrisy, and therefore hypocrisy and deceit are legitimized. Their goal, they proclaim, is to live and to let live, to achieve whatever possible, despite some limitations, in a society which, though oppressive, makes a show before world opinion of attempting to relieve their lot.

My truth, they say, is no private truth; for whether I intend it or not, each statement that I make rebounds upon them, inevitably saddles them with responsibilities which they do not want—responsibilities of explaining me away, of apologizing for my actions, and refuting me to their liberal friends. More precisely, however, they are angered because the cabinets which they have attempted to palm off on a naive society have not enough shelves to hold the likes of me. The stereotypes which they have attempted to foster are negated by me, one of their own, and my most treacherous act has been my refusal to be pigeonholed, to be categorized. Therefore, perhaps all the stereotypes are false, all the cabinets obsolete, and perhaps there are, out in that unknown where men plot murder by street light, more desperate men than myself.

"In the whole world no poor devil is lynched, no wretch is tortured, in whom I too am not degraded and murdered," writes Aimé Cesaire, voicing a truth which my friends have never deigned to explore. They do not yet realize that their fate is inseparably bound with the fate of those who suffer in every ghetto in America and that, in reality, in the minds of those who oppress others, cabinets are composed of one shelf and one shelf only. And in such a society where life can be so disregarded and humanity so often negated, no life, no humanity, is safe.

These are facts which my friends must eventually acknowledge whether they rationalize me away or not. They cannot, anyway, totally exile me from their minds, for to do so would be to deny too important a part of their private selves. My sickness is also their sickness, and because they too are sick, they are more capable of recognizing mine. In time, perhaps they will realize that the cabinets which they have constructed were predicated upon myth and fancy and that the New Negro, born of the Booker T. Washington stereotype, was a futile attempt to refute that terrible creature harbored in the dark caverns of their own minds—a creature as strange and as incomprehensible as I.

6

NAT TURNER AND
THE BLACK NATIONALISTS

RALPH ELLISON'S INVISIBLE MAN returns to his underground retreat at the end of the novel, not because he is disgusted with the world, but instead because he has arrived at the conclusion that the world is impervious to change. A black intellectual searching for some meaning to his existence and endeavoring to make peace with a society which he cannot comprehend, he is forced to choose between too opposing philosophies.

One philosophy, espoused by his grandfather, is that of accommodation: play up to white folks; don't question their assumptions of superiority; never challenge their assertions about being masters of the world—in short, coexist with white folks by "yessing them to death." The other philosophy, presented by the character Ras, the Destroyer, is nationalism: white men are the natural enemies of black people, and only by removing them from the ghettos can black men build a viable and fruitful society. Whites must therefore be driven from the ghettoes and the economic, educational and social systems placed in the hands of Blacks.

The accommodationist philosophy was espoused by Booker T. Washington, "the first *Negro leader* chosen by white people" (italics mine); and Washington's philosophy, though couched in more sophisticated terminology, is advocated by the "responsible Negro leaders" today. At the core of Washington's philosophy was a demand for "a piece of this earth"; ". . . while the Negro should not be deprived by unfair means of the franchise, political agitation alone (will) not save him, and . . . back of the ballot he must have property, industry, skill, intelligence, and character, and . . . no race without these elements [can] permanently succeed." Acquiescence was the only legitimate means of attaining these ends. With the same self-righteous conviction of the so-called responsible Negro leaders of today, Washington cow-towed to the conscience of white America: "Casting down your buckets among my people, helping and encouraging them as you are doing on these grounds, and to education of head, hand, and heart, you will find that they will buy your surplus land, make blossom the waste places in your fields, and run your factories."

Warming to his subject, Washington continues: "While doing this you can be sure in the future, as in the past, that you and your families will be surrounded by the most patient, faithful, law-abiding and unresentful people that the world has seen. As we have proved our loyalty to you in the past . . . so in the future, in our humble way, we shall stand by you with a devotion that no foreigner can approach, ready to lay down our lives if need be, in defense of yours, interlacing our industrial, commercial, civil, and religious life with yours in a way that shall make the interests of both races one."

An expert at the game of "playing up to white folks," Washington believed that "no white American ever thinks that any other race is wholly civilized until he wears the white man's clothes, eats the white man's food, speaks the white man's language, and professes the white man's religion."

Washington has been echoed by the accommodationist leaders of today. Carl Rowan, writer, commentator, and spokesman for "moderate Negro leaders," has written: "A Negro man who cannot express himself adequately, orally or in writing, who has not achieved anything academically, who has not developed technical or scientific skills, and who, as a result, cannot compete in this . . . economy, is not going to have racial pride, or any other kind."

Roy Wilkins, the elder statesman of accommodationist Negro leaders, has said somewhat the same: "He [the Negro] is a very old American, and he's American in his concepts. I think he is a liberal only on the race question. I mean, I think he is a conservative economically. I think he wants to hold on to gains in property and protection. I don't see him as a bold experimenter in political science or social reform."

And Whitney Young, a self-professed "responsible Negro leader," has come closest of all to rendering a modern version of Washington's *Atlanta Address*. "Now I think Negro citizens in the face of the years . . . have shown an amazing restraint and an amazing loyalty. I give you only last year as an example. Last year where you saw the March on Washington with its quiet dignity and its fervent pleading. Last year where you saw Negro parents . . . after their children were bombed in a Sunday school, remain calm and cool and continued to pray. Last year you saw in Jackson, Mississippi, Negro people in a church after their leader had been slain and after the widow of their leader addressed a meeting, a woman who had every right to hate, and she stood there and said, 'You mustn't hate, you must love.' And to see thousands of people in that audience . . . stand up and sing spontaneously . . . 'My country 'tis of thee, sweet land of liberty.' Now I don't know what simple element of testimony of faith in a system do you need on the part of people who have so little reason to have this kind of faith. . . . They have said to America, 'I believe in you.' "

Such statements by Negro leaders, past and present, have found accord in the hearts and minds of many Negroes primarily because Negroes, with few exceptions, have scorned revolution. For the most part, they have remained middle-class oriented either in actuality or in expectation. Here Jean Paul Sartre is correct: "What the American Negroes . . . want is an equality of rights which in no way implies a change of structure in the property system. They wish simply to share the privileges of their oppressor, that is, they really want a more complete integration."

To achieve a "more complete integration," moderate Negroes and their leaders were willing to settle for the formula inherent in the Christian ethic—salvation for some of the people if not all of the people. Modern-day Noahs, Negro leaders are preoccupied with saving those few who come aboard the ark with a predisposition toward acceptance of gradualism, non-violence, integration, and the Democratic Party; and who unashamedly, unabashedly, support the war in Vietnam.

Theirs is the vision of America structured not upon race but upon class, one in which Black men, degrees in hand, meet frequently with their white counterparts over lawn tennis, golf, or mahjong to discuss ways of containing the legitimate rebellions of the Black people still left deprived, victimized and oppressed in the ghettos of this country. As one such "leader" recently remarked: "I am interested in getting more Negroes into policy-making positions." When I inquired about the fate of those who could not be put into policy-making positions, he retreated to a curious version of the Darwinian doctrine.

The formula—some if not all of the people—is not the exclusive property of the middle-class Negroes and their leaders. Black Nationalists, irrespective of ideology, have long taken such a formula for their rallying cry. Marcus Garvey propounded a "Back to Africa" philosophy, yet at the base of his philosophy was a materialism, a bourgeois mentality, as trenchant as that of one of his chief opponents, A. Philip Randolph. Because Garvey, too, desired a piece of this earth, he was willing to settle for the formula couched in the Protestant Ethic.

This is equally true of other Nationalist groups. The guiding ethos of the Moors was prudence and economy: own your own business, buy Black, keep your money in the black ghettoes. This means no more than each man getting his share of the "Gross National Product," thereby sharing in the capitalist system, embracing its economics while deploring its social arrangements, unable to realize that one is merely the result of the other. It is, therefore, no accident that the best dressed, often most prosperous members of the black community are Black Nationalists, who are far more acquisitive and puritanical than the earliest white Puritan.

This dichotomy is proposed by Ralph Ellison's invisible man; he sees a world of extremes where one is forced to choose between Booker T. Washington and Marcus Garvey. But after close scrutiny the world is revealed to be one, without choice; for both men were controlled by the same ethic, both moved in the same direction, and both were bound together by the central fact that neither was willing to engage in revolution, to substitute for the formula "salvation for *some* of the people" that of "salvation for *all* of the people." Is it any wonder that a sensitive individual, caught in such a conundrum, would retreat to the safety and solitude of an underground dungeon?

The choices, however, have never been that restrictive. Like Americans in general, Ellison's protagonist was oblivious of the history of black people in America. For within that history is another philosophy, that presented dramatically in action, not words, by Nat Turner. Turner left no philosophical system—that is, no written philosophy—but his actions dictated a philosophy which transcends the power of words.

Turner engaged in a violent revolution against the institution of slavery; and yet it is not the violent revolution that is most important. Black people have engaged in violent revolution before and since. Turner is important because he attempted to destroy an oppressive system totally; he saw himself always as one of the oppressed, and his actions were undertaken in the spirit of liberty for all, with the intent of bringing freedom to all. Turner demanded destruction of the oppressive apparatus not coexistence with it, realizing, as today's moderate Negro leaders do not, that coexistence (integration) is only another way of enabling the many—though many more many—to oppress the few.

But most important, Turner was able to say that that moment in history for him and his people was the worst, therefore negating a moral and ethical scripture against violence. The laws, morals, and ethics constructed by a totalitarian society are, due to their very nature, invalid. No victim has a moral responsibility to recognize the laws of the oppressor. And, in the same way, he owes no allegiance to a moral code which he did not help to construct, about which he was not consulted, and which operates continuously to keep him in his oppressed status.

In addition, Turner's actions negate the philosophy of the late Martin Luther King. Violence, argued King, binds the oppressor and the oppressed together, robbing the victim of that nobility inherent in suffering, pushing him further from his oppressor; and worst of all the victim is psychologically damaged in the process.

Undoubtedly, there is psychological damage incurred by the victim who engages in violence, but this must be measured against the psychological damage incurred by the victim who does not.

Was it psychologically healthier, for example, for the family of Emmett Till to watch passively as men led their son away to certain death? Is it psychologically healthy for young people today to accept non-violently the excesses of a system which ravages their minds, bodies, and spirits, bringing a more lingering and painful death than that suffered by Emmett Till? Alongside the psychic damage inherent in acts of violence must be placed, especially for the victim, what Franz Fanon has called the purgative effect of violence. Which is the more damaging is a question for psychologists.

Turner was restricted by no such philosophy. From that moment when he realized that the conditions which he lived under were the worst, he became a revolutionary in the true sense of the word; he dedicated himself to the elimination of the oppressive social and political apparatus, not in the interests of a few but in the interest of all. He envisioned a revolution which would free every man in chains, enable every victim to breathe the air of freedom, and grant every man the right to choose his own destiny. Thus Turner accepted the formula which has now become the guiding ethic of the Black Power revolution: salvation for all or salvation for none.

No philosophy which does not demand change in the American power structure for the benefit of all the victims can be called revolutionary in any sense of the term. The Black Power proponent, like Nat Turner, realizes this fact, and for this reason he is the only true nihilist in twentieth-century America, believing with his heart, head, and soul that the conditions which exist at the moment are the worst.

In this way the Black Power philosophy differs from philosophies espoused by other black theoreticians, for its advocates envision a future—indeed the central meaning of the rebellion is predicated upon a future—in which the dignity of all men will have been restored. But the future is possible only after the complete and total destruction of the existing oppressive apparatus.

That the system is oppressive and has always operated to deny dignity to black people, to rob black people of any conception of themselves, of their worth, of their historical positions, and further, to deny them life, freedom of movement and choice is a point which all moderate Negro leaders readily concede. Such leaders differ only in the means to correct the abuses, to so transform the system that it will remedy all defects, make some restitution—if not to the victims, then to the sons and daughters of the victims.

Their plans are well known. One calls for an economic miracle, a Marshall plan; another for increased legal, legislative, and political action; still another for mass assaults upon the American conscience. And the majority of Afro-Americans accept one, sometimes all of these plans simultaneously, primarily because most still believe in the American Dream, remain wedded to the Christian myth, and see salvation and redemption in the rhetoric of leaders who promise a piece of this earth not for all but for a chosen few.

Few are capable of believing with Nat Turner that the conditions under which they live at this moment are the worst, for dedication to such a belief mandates revolution. Only the advocates of Black Power have arrived at this position, and thus Black Power is the only philosophy in America demanding revolution in the common interest of all black people.

The Black Power advocate seeks a higher meaning for man. He seeks a higher freedom. He seeks not only a more equal society, but a more just one; not a larger share of the fruits of production, but a more humane and precise definition of the human condition. As such, the advocates of Black Power are the champions of an ethic which goes far beyond existentialism, leading from property values to human ones, from degradation to dignity, from a preoccupation with some to a preoccupation with all. With Nat Turner, the Black Power proponent ignores the call of the Negro middle class and the Black Nationalists alike for a system which will only save some of the people, and demands instead a system in which no black men will wear chains and all black men will be free.

7

BLACK POWER AND

EXISTENTIAL POLITICS

IN THE ARTICLE "Farewell to Liberals: A Negro View," published in *The Nation* (October, 1962), Loren Miller condemns white liberals for their failure to deliver the promises implied or stated in the liberal creed. The accusation is somewhat unjustified. The failure lies not with liberals, but with the liberal philosophy born in the fertile soil of Europe and transplanted to the arid wasteland of America. This philosophy, humanistic in intent, died an unnatural death in the racist, hatefilled climate of the United States. No more justified is the accusation that all liberals are hypocritical and insincere. The facts of history are otherwise, and no useful purpose is served by distorting such facts for propagandistic ends. The failure results neither from the insincerity of liberals nor from their failure to produce the great society; rather, failure should be attributed to their historical impotence in coping with those situations and conditions inimical to the lives of Black people in America.

The Civil War has been attributed, in part, to the humanitarian ideals born in France and England during the European Renaissance. If one accepts this argument, the "battle to free the slaves" received impetus from the writings of liberal intellectuals: Rousseau, Mill and Locke. Again, the facts are somewhat different, pointing up the early schism which existed in liberal ranks—a schism which pitted white abolitionists against those of

71

liberal persuasion. The difference can be seen in the examples of two men: John Brown, an abolitionist, and Abraham Lincoln, a liberal.

John Brown probably never read Rousseau's *Social Contract;* Abraham Lincoln almost assuredly did. However, it was Brown who manned the barricades in an attempt to destroy slavery by the only means possible, whereas Lincoln was willing, even unto death, to bargain away emancipation for peace. The abolitionist spirit represented by John Brown was doomed to extinction soon after the Civil War, for liberals and abolitionists merged into one, wiping away all distinctions during the age of Booker T. Washington. It was the sons and daughters of the abolitionists who supported the Washington program with prestige and money; and it was the same abolitionists, now turned liberals, who enabled Washington to stifle any challenge to his authority.

This uniting of liberals behind a single, passive ideology accounts for their inability in the succeeding years to effect change in America in any meaningful way. Having given up the "sword and shield" of John Brown, liberals became castrated eunuchs, their power in the area of Black-white relations not much more potent than that of their Black wards. It is for this reason that during Reconstruction, when thirty-five hundred Black men, women, and children were lynched within a span of ten years, the liberal reaction was visible only in flowing, flowery rhetoric in which they condemned their fellow men from the safe distance of the university or the church.

Again, when Woodrow Wilson, an exponent of the new brand of liberalism, excluded Blacks from the body politic with as much ease as Robespierre affected when he condemned his fellow revolutionary, Danton, to the guillotine, white liberals excoriated these acts from the sanctuaries of the printing press, the public rostrum, and the church pulpit. It was not until the New Deal days of the Franklin Roosevelt administration that the liberals effectively used their power. It was during this period, also, that the major problems of Black America were enunciated and dealt with in a way which proved beneficial to both white liberals and negro leaders. For the liberals, exercising their powers, hastened to construct the welfare state, giving form and substance to the welfare state mentality which was as old as Harriet Beecher Stowe, and thus cemented a Faustian pact between negroes and themselves.

The pact offered something to each party. For whites, the programs of the welfare state made Black men dependent upon them, thus enabling liberals to pose as the benefactors of humanity—not withstanding the fact that the welfare state was overgenerous to some, criminal to many, and debilitating to most. For negroes, the pact assured a return to the days of the Freedmen's Bureau when, after slavery, the job of rehabilitation was entrusted to whites who set policy, enunciated philosophy, and charted direction. But more important, the philosophy of the welfare state created an attitude of dependence in which men placed their faith in the mystical credo that others were capable of solving their problems. Such a creed robbed Black people of the propensity for sacrifice, of the willingness to mount realistic, sustained initiatives, of the ability to make a systematic, organized attempt to construct viable communities within those areas which were, physically at least, their own. Then as now, Blacks, divided and disorganized, either retired from the battle, proposed impossible schemes, or accepted the liberal thesis of the equalitarian society based upon integration.

Integration is a concept derived from the welfare state philosophy, and its greatest success has been in destroying initiative and stifling creativity on the part of men who need to control their own destinies. Moreover, the concept of integration—like the welfare state philosophy—was one which both negro leaders and white liberals could live with. To be sure, there are white liberals who are charlatans and hypocrites; yet the essential characteristic of the white liberal is the need to save someone, preferably Black people, and integration, the best means of effecting this salvation, will transform twenty million Black men into carbon-copied white men. In such a society, in which all men were to be invisible, the humanistic principles applicable to the golden age could be operative. On the other hand, negro leaders, much more sophisticated and less naively romantic, saw integration as the instrument by which—as Stokely Carmichael has noted—selected Blacks would become card-carrying members of the American

Mainstream, while the mass would be pacified through the expansion of the welfare state.

This policy survived the years and has only recently been challenged by the concept of Black Power. Young people, in loud and uncompromising tones, have "sounded the death knell" of integration; and despite the protestations of Roy Wilkins and others of the antiquarian past, the idea of the egalitarian society in which Black men become the invisible men of the future now belongs to the cesspool of American historical thought. Integration is truly dead; and no more glorious a death has occurred since Adolf Hitler put a bullet into his own brain.

The death of integration, however, threatens to split the Black Power movement apart. In part this is due to the long years of the success of the welfare state ideology, which, transforming men into children, has made them subservient to the liberal fathers' image. Thus, the situation is analogous to that of a young child taken from his mother at an early age; such a rupture causes extreme frustration. The child may sulk in his special corner, bemoaning the passing of the comfortable old days; he may lash out in uncontrolled fury, mouthing slogans and shouting abusive epithets; or, close to the breaking point, he may dream impossible dreams to replace those of happier days.

This analogy between the child and many Black Power proponents is intentional. For many, incapable of accepting the concept of Black Power and all that the concept entails, have retreated to the sanctuary of "their piece of earth," there to brood about the past. Others, more distraught, excoriate "whitey" from one speaker's platform to another, "whipping that boy," to use Ralph Ellison's phrase, piling abuse upon abuse on the head of their favorite "honky."

Nowhere are these attitudes exhibited more blatantly than in some of the literature of the Black Power era. Some Black writers propound the most mystical of philosophies in poems, short stories, and plays, and their meanings are completely incomprehensible to everyone—one suspects even to the writers themselves. Others continue to present the same old stock characters, the same old plots, and the same old situations with the added dimensions of the theme "Black is beautiful."

Out of their frustrations, these writers have failed to realize that what is beautiful is the lives of Black people recorded simply, without mysticism, but with truth, and that the beauty of the Black spirit in this, the most oppressive of societies, is not only fertile ground for the writer to explore, but also the material from which he must construct and codify the theorems of a Black Aesthetic. For we are today in a Black cultural renaissance, in which, for perhaps the last time, Black Nationalist writers will be able to project—to Black people—a sense of our unique, separate cultural identity by resolving the dichotomy between art and function, thereby making art functional and relevant to the Black community.

But, too, there are the dreamers. Those who, incapable of confronting the world as it is, dream of the world as it should have been years ago. They are the octogenarians of the race, conjurors of old, outmoded ideas. Their greatest virtue is optimism; their greatest fault is ignorance combined with an arrogant disrespect for the intelligence of Black people. One needs no college degree to realize that Black Power is a goal yet to be attained, and that the Black masses, having been sold down the river by race charlatans so often in the past, will adopt no new philosophy without ample cause.

The dreamer, however, unlike the masses of Black people, believes that Black Power has been obtained. Moreover, he believes that he and his group have been instrumental in bringing this about. Therefore, if one accepts this misguided analysis, the dreamer is justified in condemning Black men of differing persuasion, of demanding that all Black men join him and his organization, and ordering that those who refuse be lined "up against the wall."

The reality is, however, that the goal of Black Power has not been attained. Were Black Power an actuality, Adam Clayton Powell would have his seniority in Congress; John Hatchett would be directing the Martin Luther King Center at N.Y.U.; John Carlos would not have been dismissed from the Olympic team; and the Mayor of the City of New York would not be cowtowing to the racist-oriented United Federation of Teachers. Therefore, despite the fact that there are Blacks who are hindrances to the movement, no organization has accomplished enough to warrant the right to assign such men to the wall.

But dreams, as Sigmund Freud noted long ago, are wish fulfillments; and all Black men at some time have dreamed the impossible dream. What Black man has not imagined himself a Toussaint L'Ouverture doing to the Americans what the Haitians did to the French? What Black man, if he is honest with himself, has not dreamed of mass murder, of burning his way across America in an expedition that would make Sherman's march to the sea insignificant by comparison? And what Black man has not wished, deep in his private soul, that his people were the Viet Cong?

The awful truth of the matter is that Black people are not the Viet Cong. Despite the argument that "this is my land, too," this land belongs to the Indians, who are as powerless as Black people to dispel the invaders; and though the Viet Cong will eventually expel the invader from their soil, no such action is possible in the case of Blacks in America. Therefore, the revolution, which the rhetoricians tell us is on the way, can result in one thing and one thing only—the systematic extermination of Black people as a race.

Here the dreamers display that characteristic ignorance which stems from a lack of knowledge of history. For, behind their rhetoric lies the old belief in the potency of white liberalism and the philosophy of the benevolent state. They believe that, in the final analysis, either sympathetic whites in America, or non-whites of the Third World, or both, will prevent white Americans from carrying out the final solution. This, despite the fact that the Third World has yet to come to the aid of the Viet Cong, the Black South Africans, or Black Rhodesians; despite the fact that liberals have proven themselves, over the years, incapable of mustering any weapons more powerful than prayer and songs when Black life has been at stake. The truth is that we stand alone; and a nation capable of exterminating the Indians, putting Haitians into concentration camps, and lynching over a half million Blacks is not only quite capable of executing a large portion of the twenty million Blacks in this country, but capable also of *carrying out* such an act and *legitimizing* it throughout the world. Here is the evidence of real power—the power to control men, not by tanks and guns, but by the supremacy of the mass media, the domination of the instruments of propaganda, and control of the educational institutions, which are used to destroy one truth and replace it with another. American society is unique in this respect. It manufactures people as it manufactures things. Its power stems, not from its vast military might, but instead from its ability to convince the victim that he deserves the punishment which it metes out. The white establishment, therefore, is not the classic example of the historical oppressor; for Blacks are controlled much more in a psychological than a physical sense, and one can not fight ideas with Molotov cocktails.

The dreamers aside, Black people may indeed have to fight—given the intransigence of American society, the shift towards the right which will intensify once the Viet Cong victory is assured, and the racism which pervades every institution of American society. And if fight we must, then fight we will. But there is no room for romanticism; we will fight alone, and there will be no victors.

But neither will there be a victory attained in pursuit of the "New Colonization"—a thesis set forward by an increasingly large number of Blacks. That many Black people have been willing to leave America for other countries is a fact as old as Paul Cuffee, a wealthy Black shipowner who used his wealth and his ships to transport Blacks out of America. In addition, in the nineteenth century and well into the twentieth, the argument for colonization was so strong among Black people that hardly an issue of *The Anglo-American, Freedom's Journal,* or Douglass' paper failed to contain some article or letter to the editor on the subject.

The new version of the colonization theme proposes that America set aside a number of states for the exclusive use of Black people. Thus one of the most expansionist nations in history, one which fought a war on its own soil to prevent white people from walking away with several states, is somehow to be coerced or persuaded to give away one fifth of its territory to Blacks. But no nation has ever given up its territory unless forced to do so. And there is, as of yet, no power on the horizon which seems capable of exerting enough pressure on the power establishment of America to force them to destroy the physical solidarity of this country.

This is not to condemn those who forward such proposals. It is to demand evaluation of such proposals in light of what Black Power, in its short history, has meant in terms of Black liberation, as well as what it must mean as a political instrument for the future. And here, of course, is the central problem. The breakdown of the old white liberal-negro coalition has placed Black people in the most existential position of their lives. For the first time, Blacks are demanding real change, not the semblance of change, real power, not the illusion of power, and are attempting to construct real, viable alternatives to the programs of the past.

The death of God, wrote Nietzsche, means that man was thrown back upon himself. Concomitantly, the death of integration means that Blacks are thrown back upon themselves, forced to forge from the smithy of their Black souls the theories, forms, and institutions by which Black people are "to live or to die." This is, to be sure, an existential undertaking; for Black Power, in its realistic manifestations is an existential doctrine. The weight of survival has been placed upon the shoulders of Blacks, and only Blacks can determine their future.

That Black people are capable of this task needs no comment. We can build our communities and transform them into working, livable units. The only requirement is a complete break with the philosophy of the welfare state. For men who believe in the benevolence of government can not believe in their own power; for them the politics of existentialism becomes the politics of dependence.

But the task requires, in addition, that Black theoreticians talk sense to Black people, that they tell it like it really is, that they bring home the hard cold pragmatic facts of the situation in which we find ourselves at this stage. To control our communities is no easy task. We need not rhetoricians, but architects, planners and builders; not fire and brimstone orators, but teachers, entrepreneurs, historians and all that vast paraphernalia essential to the realistic operation and control of a community.

Such theoreticians must demand that our children get an

education—as minimal as that may be—in the existing institutions, until such time as we have either transformed those institutions or created our own. They must demand that Black people be presented with the whole picture, and that the charlatan and the hustler be brought to task. They must criticize those who offer the wornout theories of the past, as well as those whose satisfaction (sexual?) is derived from orgiastic, meaningless attacks upon "whitey"—attacks totally irrelevant to the problems at hand.

There must be a re-evaluation of values which entails a final and complete break with the liberal orthodoxy and methodology of the past. There must be total destruction of the welfare state and the welfare state mentality; the best in men must be called forth, and it must be demanded that Black men expend as much creative energy in building the Black community as they have expended throughout history in attempting to become good Americans. None of this is easy. Such undertakings entail frustration, bitterness, and disillusion. Yet sacrifice of the highest order is a necessary requirement: sacrifice and a dedication to Black people, not just to Blackness, which means more than wearing a natural hair-do or a dashiki. The dedication must be to race. There must be an unashamed, unabashed commitment to race that admits the differences between Blacks and whites, and explores these differences.

This means that it is more important to write a Black novel than an American novel, more important to support a Black institution than a white one, more important to address Black problems than American problems. But above all, it is most important to realize that as an existential doctrine, Black Power demands the allegiance of men who are capable of transcending the past and challenging the future. For only such men can possibly confront the dangerous era that lies ahead.

> The old year is dying in the
> night/ring out wild bells and
> let him die.

8

BLACK POWER OR

BLACK FASCISM?

On a hot dusty road in Mississippi during the summer of 1966, men, women, and children—victims the night before of ruthless white power—responded to the question "What do you want?" of a courageous black leader with the refrain "Black Power." Two years after this historic occurrence the phrase Black Power has given impetus to a new kind of revolution, involving—as numerous Black Power conferences have shown—Blacks of all ideologies and persuasions. The revolution is discernible in such distant places as Mississippi, where young children tutored by members of S.N.C.C. are pursuing black awareness, and the college campuses of America, where black students are presenting instructors and officials with demands based upon Black Power concepts.

The revolution has been a long time coming. As far back as 1963 many of today's "militants" were still seeking the goals ardently pursued then as now by "responsible Negro leaders." Carried away by the rhetoric of the times, the slogans "Freedom Now" and "We Shall Overcome," and mesmerized by the seeming victories won through adherence to non-violence and the pursuit of integration, even many of those who were realists found themselves caught up in a Kafkaesque world in which reality gave way to illusion.

Yet the psychedelic state could not long remain. Reality—

never far away—was revealed once the movement turned towards the North, towards the homes, jobs, and schools of those liberal proponents who, their voices raised as one with Blacks, had sung enthusiastically to Southern bigots: "We shall overcome." And once a commitment to see this reality was made, changes of far-reaching import were demanded and sought by young men who, unlike their parents, refused to chase that romantic illusion, an integrated society.

Many had refused to see the situation as it really was until after the "March on Washington." As thousands of black people went to the shrine of the gods, offering libation and penance, many who had stayed away began to realize that neither God nor Government would grant relief to an impotent army invading its domain with weapons no more powerful than spirituals and ministerial salvos to a non-existent white God. And they noted, too, that the black people participating in the March on Washington represented less than one-fifth of one percent of black people in the country—a statistic which illustrates that even before the Integrationist-Nationalist debate was brought into the open by Black Power, the majority of black people preferred not integration but security, not Black-white brotherhood but food and education for their children, not assimilation (a means of transforming twenty million people into invisible men) but the means of living a decent life.

But it was in the aftermath of the March that many gained their most penetrating insight into the civil rights movement. Black people are not novices oblivious to the machinations of power politics. Our history has been filled with chauvinists and Uncle Toms who have allied themselves with white power in pursuit of selfish goals. Yet we were so mesmerized in the fifties that we ignored the lessons of the past. The March on Washington was a sobering reminder, pointing up the fact that the past was indeed very much with us, that Booker T. Washington was not yet dead, and that Negro power allied with white power could still be used to stifle dissent, to mute any voice which did not accept illusion as God-granted reality.

If the proceedings leading to this revelation had not been so serious, they would be ironic and pathetic—the stuff of which good comedy is made. There was the spectacle of Roy Wilkins, bowing his head, raising his arms, pointing in the direction of the buildings which housed Congress, and shouting to the absent congressmen (presumably the Southerners): "Give us enough time and we will liberate you, too."

It was to be discovered much later, however, that Wilkins and his associates, who had chided the country for denying freedom to Black people, had joined in an endeavor to deny freedom to one of their own colleagues. In the *New York Times* on the day following the March, there was a column dealing with a "rights leader" who had been forced to delete parts of the speech he had prepared for the March. John Lewis, the chairman of S.N.C.C., had planned to allude to the coming revolution which would burn its way across the nation, and in protest against this passage, some of the white participants threatened to pack their bags and go home, leaving the Afro-Americans to carry on their own show.

Rather than allow the white participants to withdraw from sponsorship, the "responsible Negro Leaders" chose to deny freedom to John Lewis—that is, they forced him to delete from his prepared text the passages considered offensive to whites. In so doing, white and Negro power were used in the most tyrannical manner. Once again, it was demonstrated that the historical alignment between Negroes and white liberals, which Booker T. Washington began in earnest, continued to dictate the tone, direction, and goals of black people in America, primarily by silencing dissent and neutralizing opposition.

Yet the angry words which came forth from the men, women, and children during the "Meredith March" have proved immune to such coordinated efforts of white and Negro power. Despite the attempts by both civil rights leaders and white liberals to silence the proponents of Black Power in black churches, colleges, lodge halls and the ghettoes, Black Power has become a viable movement in which people of all persuasions have come together in a common undertaking.

No idea in America has caught the imagination of so many black people in so short a time, brought awareness to individuals in so many different strata of life, and provoked responses and programs from so many people of diverse talents. It would seem that at this point—to use an old cliché—the only thing that Black Power has to fear is Black Power itself.

At a recent seminar on Black Power, a young student put the following question to a panel: "I believe in Blackness, but I don't identify with Africa, and there are other black people who do not. Does this mean that I can't take part in the revolution?" The young lady was searching for answers. Like so many, she was unaware of what to do in these momentous times.

No one, however, attempted to answer her question. With few exceptions, the panel was convinced of its own righteousness—as if some black god had ordained it with the power to speak the truth for twenty million people. The only answer forthcoming was not really an answer at all, but a number of clichés. "You have been brainwashed by white people," the panel declared, and "want to deny your black heritage"—statements which proved that the panel had little understanding of the central issues of Black Power and was substituting emotionalism for reason and understanding.

Such has long been a characteristic of the fascist mind. Fascism as an ideology preys upon the purported ignorance of the people in the belief that all the people are ignorant. The emotional fascist, therefore, has no respect for the minds of other men, is convinced of their inferiority, and appeals to them only on the grounds of irrationality. Fascism is an important aspect of white power. John Lewis was denied the freedom to present his views because men believed that he should not think for himself; and the young student was attacked because men believed that she should have no opinion different from their own.

Such fascists have nothing but contempt for the people, though they attempt to compensate by sporting "au naturels" and dashikis. Like Father Divine, they believe that black people can be moved only through emotionalism, and that the man who shouts the loudest is the wisest, best informed and best suited for leadership. They have only recently discovered that Africa is not a land ruled by Tarzan but instead by black men like themselves, and that civilizations existed in Africa long before Columbus discovered America. Still, they berate others who have not yet discovered this; and instead of attempting to enlighten these others, they assume, *a priori*, like their white counterparts, that "them niggers can't learn anyway."

In addition, emotional fascists have a contempt for planning. Understanding neither revolution nor the nature of black people in this country, they do not believe that we are capable of sustaining a social revolution. Not understanding the nature of white power, they are opposed to any long-range planning. What they want, they shout, is a violent revolution, not tomorrow but today, and they encourage young people to go out and "take care of business."

Yet they have taken care of no business themselves. Like the Negro leaders, the emotionalists are the last to know what is going on in the black ghettoes—because they listen to no voices but their own—and the first to leap under the bed when the action starts. They have the courage for one kind of action, and that is to shout "get whitey" and "hate whitey" slogans to people who are beginning to realize that shouting such slogans is as useless a preoccupation as shouting "we shall overcome" from the speaker's stand in front of the Washington monument. Perhaps, as one such individual told me, I do not know what Black Power is: I do know, however, what it is not; it is neither white fascism nor religious fanaticism.

But as dangerous as the emotional fascist may be, he is not so dangerous as the Professional Black Nationalist, who shows the same contempt for the people, but on a more sophisticated plane. The Professional Nationalist is the Black-by-Night missionary coming into the ghetto after sundown and intimidating others with his "more militant than thou" attitude. He has read Fanon—although he does not understand him—shuffled through a few pages of Guevara, knows something about Garvey—though not the whole story—and quotes Malcolm verbatim. This superficial machinery is designed to prove his militancy; yet, in effect, it allows him to serve as a liaison between the black community uptown and The Man downtown. He has discovered, finally, that it pays to be Black, and he capitalizes on his blackness to the utmost. No man is blacker than he, none more dedicated to the "cause of the people," none has a better solution. He will disrupt the gatherings of others and even threaten their lives (today some black leaders who, unlike the "responsible Negro leaders," venture into the ghettos armed, not to protect themselves from the C.I.A. but from other Blacks).

The Professional Nationalist is also the professional fascist. He is not interested in persuading men to accept his point of view through reason and logic—since his point of view differs little from The Man's. Instead, he hopes to establish a totalitarian apparatus wherein all proposals will be subject to his authority. He is not opposed to planning, for he has come to realize that there is money in planning; but he opposes any plan which he does not originate, sponsor and dictate.

Central to both the emotional and the professional fascist is their anti-intellectualism. The intellectual is always a danger to the fascist mind because the intellectual demands the right to think for himself. S.N.C.C. changed its orientation from integration to Black Power because Carmichael demanded the right to think for himself, to say things not sanctioned by the white and Negro power structure. We know how that power structure has reacted. It has not attempted to debate the issues fairly and squarely with black people, nor has it been willing to bring its ideas before black people in a serious attempt at honest discussion.

This is because the fascist mind, basically weak and insecure, can not deal with issues through logic, reason, and persuasion. The black fascists are no different, and in this respect they are joined by some black leaders. They fear that the intellectual will take over their movement and render them impotent as leaders. In other words the black intellectual is as feared as the bubonic plague.

There are historical reasons for such fears. Black intellectuals have usually joined the civil rights struggle on the side of the integrationists. Too often they have pocketed their degrees, moved away from the ghetto, joined the N.A.A.C.P., and sold their skills and talents to the highest bidder, usually white. But this is equally true of most of Black America before the Black Power movement. Most black men were caught up in the integrationist bag, seeing salvation only in terms of what Negro and white leaders said that it was. Whether or not the black intellectual deserves more opprobrium than the rest of us is open to question.

The black fascists are not opposed to intellectuals for these reasons. Men who are searching for personal power, whether through fantasy or political dealings with the power structure, they are opposed to those who have the ability to propose plans, methods, and goals different from their own. They refuse to understand that the intellectual, owing his allegiance to the people, must serve as a critic deriving his ideas from the people and putting them forth in favor of the people.

This, the black fascist cannot understand. Neither can he understand the guiding ethos of every revolution from the French to the Algerian—that ideas are to be debated, then accepted or discarded not as a result of threats or emotional intimidation, but instead through working in an atmosphere of mutual respect and cooperation, realizing that in the area of truth there are no final dicta handed down by impotent gods.

The men, women, and children in Mississippi realized this fact. In the face of the most awesome power—the white Mississippi police and National Guard—they dared to choose Black Power. They did not choose the power which but a few hours before had denied them the right to express themselves in the way they deemed best; they did not choose the self-righteous power of narrowminded, frustrated, paranoic, insecure little men whose only answer to any plea for understanding was a barrage of empty clichés and nonsensical epithets; they did not choose the power of those who attempted to persuade them, through sophisticated rhetoric, that they and only they had found the road to salvation.

They voted in favor of a free and open society in which men would come together, debate the issues, and sort out their differences, not as bewildered children, helpless without the sound of the master's voice, but as conscientious men truly concerned with their own destiny. Theirs was the spirit which dared to thunder forth in the face of oppression—while staring into the gun barrels of the oppressor: "We want Black Power!" Black Power and not Black Fascism.

And those of us who feel akin to this spirit have no recourse but to insist that it is Black Power which they shall have. We must demand this regardless of the consequences, for if the fascists are allowed to take over a movement begun by sincere and honest people, then we will have not Black Power but Black Fascism, differing in no respect from the white fascism against which Blacks have fought and died throughout our history in this country. At this point, it will then be incumbent upon those of us who are determined to destroy white fascism to oppose this carbon copy; for fascism must be opposed at all costs, whether it be white or Black.

9

"HELL NO,

BLACK MEN

WON'T GO!"

AT THE HEIGHT OF the protest against the war in Vietnam in the summer of 1967, two black soldiers on active duty in the battle zone appeared before the television cameras of the nation's major networks. Presumably, their appearance was to undermine the Negroes, here at home, who urge other Negroes of draft age not to participate in the war. This function was to be performed by rebutting two nationally known Negro leaders who had consistently urged black men to answer their draft calls with the refrain, "Hell no, we won't go!"

Stokely Carmichael and the late Martin Luther King were the two leaders who most exemplified the Negro's opposition to the war in Vietnam. To many whites they have been the apotheosis of black resistance, and each has received insults, and threats of physical violence. However, the public viewed the two men quite differently. Carmichael was seen as a young, intellectual iconoclast; a hero out of the pages of Malraux's revolutionary novel, *Man's Fate*—a nihilist whose rashness knows no boundaries.

The view of Dr. King was exactly the opposite. Neither rash nor iconoclastic, and certainly not an intellectual, he was seen as a mild-mannered, reasonable, though impatient, Negro, embodying at times within his own person that moral fiber of which Blacks are supposedly constructed.

To rebut men whose ideals are so different, whose images, in the public mind, are so contrary, men had to be selected with consummate skill; chosen, not as the result of fortuitous fate, but as anti-images—as antagonists even—in order to effectively counteract what one correspondent has called, "the dangerous thinking of some American Negroes." Carmichael and King could be rebutted only by authentic, in-the-flesh heroes, men in the battle areas of Vietnam, doing their utmost for God, mother, and country.

The first soldier resembled Stokely Carmichael in everything except anger and rashness. Young, handsome, and vocal, attired in war gear, he was the perfect foil, and his pronouncements did the nation justice: No, he did not agree with Stokely Carmichael. His country was at war, and as a loyal American it was his duty to defend his country. Of course he was concerned about things at home, but after his experiences in Vietnam with people who thought of him as "just people," he knew that America would work out its problems at home. The important thing was that he had a job to do here, and he was determined to do it.

The foil for Dr. King was, naturally, a soldier of higher rank and educational status. A captain in the army, member of the N.A.A.C.P. in civilian life, mature, and apparently intelligent; he wished that people like Martin Luther King would realize the harm they do to their country's image. The country was engaged in a vicious war against communism, and every American should support that war. He was an American, and the enemies of his country were his enemies and the enemies of black people. Moving beyond this, the Captain aimed a few verbal blasts at the rioters in the nation's ghettoes: Though things were bad in some parts of the country, riots were not a way of making things better. Negroes had to have more initiative, more concern for their own welfare, and they should not be influenced by demagogues—those who help to cause riots, and who tell them not to support the war in Vietnam.

As a black man, my first response to these two spokesmen was to question the lack of opportunity for soldiers of differing persuasions and temperament to air their views. If my information is correct, there are many black soldiers who do not share the views of these two men. On reflection, it became clear that the job of these two men was simply to rebut two popular figures in the black community, not in an attempt to appeal to Black America, but rather to appease and comfort white America.

America is a country in which comfort is more important than anything else and the statements of Carmichael and King regarding the Vietnam conflict have caused extreme discomfort. It is not comforting to know that a large number of black men would prefer to die fighting tyranny, oppression, hunger and disease in the black ghettoes of America than to die in the jungles of Vietnam for an abstract freedom for the Vietnamese.

An increasing number of white people—even articulate and dedicated members of the liberal community—are becoming incensed upon realizing that black men are not really grateful to the country which, according to eminent commentators on the American scene, has provided them with a higher standard of living than that enjoyed by any other black people on earth. Such ingratitude distorts the image of an America constantly attempting, against historical odds, to live up to those ideals upon which it was founded.

To uphold these ideals and to assure white Americans a reasonable amount of mental comfort, the two soldiers in Vietnam were brought into the nation's living rooms, serving that function which Negro leaders have served so adequately before, pacification of the American conscience. Such is the mentality of white people regarding black people; that a single Negro, echoing the words which find accord in white America's own breast, is taken as the metaphor for all Blacks—the spokesman who has really told it like it is.

This is no new phenomenon. Dick Gregory's idea of the "Hertz Rent-A-Negro Corporation," through which Negroes would be rented out to white people to tell them what other Negroes believe, is less a joke than a practiced reality. For a long time, white America has had at its disposal a cadre of Negroes whose function is to soothe the American conscience, to assure white Americans that things are not as bad as a few "irrational and irresponsible" Negroes would have them appear to be. Such Negroes serve America in much the same way that the *deus ex machina* served Greek theatergoers—as a reminder that things could never degenerate to the point of no resolution, and that, in the final analysis, good, justice, and reason would prevail.

The Negro who tells white America what it wants to hear has always been with us. Against the rational polemic of W.E.B. DuBois, Booker T. Washington came forth to articulate the "real problem"; advocating in his "Atlanta Exposition Address" the program which the white South had long before conceived and begun to implement. Against the postulations of Marcus Garvey, A. Philip Randolph became a constant scene-stealer, assuring America at every turn that, despite Garvey's enormous following, Negroes were immune to the attractions of Black Nationalism.

Malcolm X and the Black Muslims were subjected to perhaps the most serious scathing of all, drawing thunderous phrases of denunciation from established Negro leaders as well as some not yet established. An examination of the rhetoric of such leaders during the Malcolm X years will convince even the most disinterested observer that Negro leaders, reflecting white concern, had nominated Malcolm X public enemy number one. (This is understandable, though hardly excusable: it is a fact that when white people become paranoiac, some Negro leaders become hysterical, and proceed to act accordingly.)

Recent events prove that the Negro who tries to assuage the fears of whites is still in great demand. When Stokely Carmichael uttered the phrase, "Black Power," during the Meredith March, the words had hardly faded away before Negro leaders were beamed into every living room in the nation. So all-pervasive was the hysteria at this point, that even non-black leaders like Vice President Humphrey felt compelled to join the fray—pacifying white America by offering assurances that black people would not take this step into "romanticism and murder."

During the teachers' strike in New York City in 1967, many black people, myself among them, joined with the Afro-American Teacher's Association in protesting the strike. Then, when the grievances of the Black community were articulated by such spokesmen as Floyd McKissick, H. Rap Brown, Charles Kenyatta, and Jesse Gray, the United Federation of Teachers dug into its files and brought forth its personal Negro leader; tired, old, metaphysical Bayard Rustin, whose following in the Black community numbers less than three.

Again, when Negro athletes agreed not to participate in the coming Olympic Games, the white press reached back into the past, dragging forth such now forgotten "Leaders" as Jesse Owens, Don Newcombe, and the perennial expert on Negro sports and sportsmen, Joe Louis, to assure America that the majority of Negro athletes did not hold such radical views and would not interject "politics into the sports arena."

Yet the most recent event demanding the continual involvement of the Negro leaders has been the war in Vietnam. Almost daily, "responsible leaders" of the Young-Wilkins variety are paraded before the American public, their statements taken as gospel by the American people—despite evidence to the contrary —much in the way that the statements of the two soldiers were taken as evidence that the overwhelming majority of black people in America support the Administration's Vietnam policies; and that the statement made by Stokely Carmichael before nine hundred cheering students and faculty members in a speech at Hampton Institute in 1967—"Hell no, we won't go!"—represents little more than emotionalism, irrationalism, and youthful iconoclasm, completely lacking any basis in fact, and inapplicable to most black Americans.

But still, more and more black men in the ghettos are deciding that they will not go to the war in Vietnam, and their decisions are not the result of emotionalism nor youthful iconoclasm. Not only are their decisions derived from first-hand experience of the treatment received by them and their kinsmen at the hands of present-day white Americans; they are even more aware of the history of the participation of black men in past American wars and the treatment accorded these men and their fellow Negroes once those wars had ended.

It is ironic that the first man gunned down by the British redcoats was a black man. Crispus Attucks was, however, only one of the many Blacks who sacrificed their lives in the Revolutionary War for a freedom and liberty which their survivors and descendants would never know. Some of these men served as proxies for their masters, others were released from slavery specifically to take part in the war.

The decision to allow Negroes to participate in the war at all was reached only after serious deliberation. General George Washington, who at the outset had wanted no black soldiers at all, relented to the point of accepting freed Negroes in his Revolutionary Army. His decree was soon amended, however, when Americans realized that many Negroes were escaping from slavery to join the British because the British promised them manumission. America followed suit, promising black men who participated in the war that, after the war, their freedom would be assured. Thus began the first of a long series of broken promises made to black men by white men; for once the war was over, many of the men who had joined in the fight for American independence were reenslaved.

This breach of faith did not prevent Frederick Douglass from petitioning President Lincoln, during the Civil War, to accept black soldiers into the Union Army. Douglass saw the war between the states—despite evidence to the contrary—as a war to end slavery. But like Washington before him, President Lincoln, too, was reluctant to use black soldiers. He was not eager to "loose that black hand" which Douglass claimed lay impotent; not willing, that is, to allow black men to kill white men, even in the interest of liberty. Only under the steady prodding of Douglass, and as a result of Confederate victories, did Lincoln finally accept Negro soldiers—at less pay, with fewer supplies, under segregated conditions—into his army.

The men fought well despite these handicaps, earning the respect of many of their commanders in the field. However, once the war was over, they became a part of that displaced mass of black people, soon to be deserted by the very union forces they had aided. Left to the mercy, caprices, and devices of those whom they had fought against, their fight for liberty was, in the final analysis, no more than a fight for reenslavement, this time by the "Black Code Laws"—chains more binding than those welded about their arms and ankles by callous masters.

Yet when the world plunged into its first global war, W.E.B. DuBois urged black men to close ranks and fight shoulder to shoulder with their white brothers in a common cause. This cause —"to make the world safe for democracy"—was a cause which so astute a scholar as DuBois must have certainly suspected.

For President Woodrow Wilson had never even attempted to make America safe for democracy. Almost from the inception of his administration he had begun to transform the nation's capital into the most segregated city outside of the deep South. Overnight the civil services were resegregated, "colored" rest rooms were established in office buildings, restaurants, and government establishments; and the lynching rate climbed as high as two Blacks per month.

Despite Wilson's reputed declaration that "this is a white man's war," there was little resistance this time to accepting black troops. In fact, the editor of the "Waterberry Times" considered the use of black men a good thing: "It seems a pity to waste good white men in battle with such a foe. The cost of sacrifice would be nearly equalized were the job assigned to Negro troops. . . . An army of nearly a million could probably be easily recruited from the Negroes of this country without drawing from its industrial strength or commercial life. . . . We will be sacrificing white blood . . . and drawing our skilled labor when unskilled labor was available."

Still black men heeded the call to participate in the "war to end all wars," serving in segregated units, most of them under the control of Southern officers, one of whom welcomed his troops with the following words: "[You] need not expect democratic treatment . . . White men made the division, and they can break it just as quickly if it becomes a troublemaker. . . . Don't go where your presence is not desired."

The only place, it seemed, that the presence of black soldiers was desired was the battlefield. In America, their presence quickly became a signal for danger. Trained as men, the soldiers proceeded to act as such, rioting and even killing, retaliating against acts of barbarism directed against them, despite the uniforms they wore. When drum-major Noble Sissle of the 15th New York Infantry was assaulted by a group of white men for refusing to take off his army-issued hat in the presence of a white newspaper dealer, rumors of war swept Spartanburg, South

Carolina, warning that the coming war was to be fought, not against the Germans, but against the enemy closer to home. The 15th was made a part of the 369th Regiment, another contingent of black soldiers, and immediately shipped to the front.

Once again, black men proved their valor, winning a considerable share of the victories, and receiving many decorations both individually and collectively. One such decoration was France's *Croix de Guerre*, awarded to foreign troops for the first time. Lauding the black soldiers at this important ceremony, the French commander remarked: "You have won the greatest battle in history and saved the most sacred cause, the liberty of the world. . . . Posterity will be indebted to you with gratitude."

Perhaps posterity will repay its debt. But it seems evident that America will not. Hardly had the victory parade down New York's Fifth Avenue ended before the Ku Klux Klan arose, stronger than ever, to take advantage of a world now made safe for democracy. In the same year in which the war ended, seventy-six Negroes, many still in uniform, were lynched. That following year—one of those now forgotten hot summers of American history—Blacks were the recipients of America's indebtedness in Texas, Arkansas, Pennsylvania, Washington, and Chicago, Illinois where in a twelve-day massacre, black men, women, and children were maimed and murdered by mobs of whites, operating with tacit assistance from the legal authorities.

These facts notwithstanding, in World War II, black men went forth once again, though with mixed emotions, to defend the freedom of their country. And this despite the fact that lynchings had now become an accepted part of the American Character, so much so that an antilynching bill could not be passed in the Congress even though the rate of lynchings had gone up during the Roosevelt years to one per week.

Once again black men acquitted themselves well on the field of battle; and once again after the battle was done, their heroism and sacrifice was forgotten. After helping to defeat the racist regime of Adolf Hitler, Americans returned to a position, vis-à-vis their fellow citizens, as severe as that of the Nazi racists. Black people were the first to be dismissed from the defense jobs, the last to receive training for the coming years of automation, still segregated in housing and public accommodations, and still victims of the rope, the torch, the firebomb, and the rifle at the hands of white Americans North and South.

Nor did the situation change after Korea. Black veterans returning to America found that they and their people were in the same predicament as before; still the recipients of inferior education, the worst jobs, the most degrading treatment, and still subject to acts of terrorism, physical assault, and murder. In exchanging the khaki brown for civilian clothes, they discovered what the compatriots of Crispus Attucks had discovered after the Revolutionary War—that the most cherished freedom which they had fought to preserve was the freedom of Americans to oppress them and their people.

This is a terrible truth to arrive at concerning one's country. And yet nothing, either in the past or in the present, has made it necessary for black people to disavow this truth; and if indeed the future is merely a product of past and present, then the black soldiers fighting and dying in Vietnam—including the two Negro representatives—can look forward to a future differing very little from that of their predecessors. Their people will still be oppressed, still given the worst jobs, their children still forced to attend inferior schools, and most of them still forced to live in crime-infested ghettos. They will continually be the victims of acts of violence—no longer the sole expression of the Ku Klux Klan, but now initiated by solid citizens, those of the suburbs of Chicago, Boston, Newark, and New York City, who will rationalize their actions with the assertion that they are fighting to preserve *their freedom.*

The Congress of the United States will reflect the consensus of such constituents and refuse to pass civil rights legislation, except the most meaningless kind; veto rat bills; dismiss a black congressman with impunity; cut appropriations funds; refuse to enact open housing legislation—in short, refuse to accord Negroes, who have fought and died for this country, the elemental rights which it accords any fair-skinned foreigner who steps off any boat in New York City's harbor.

In addition, there is the fact that the most fervent supporters of the war in Vietnam are men and organizations whose names read like a Who's Who of racism in America: Congressmen East-land, Thurmond, Rivers, and Stennis; Governors Wallace, Faubus, and Maddox; the Conservative Party, the American Nazi Party, the John Birch Society, and the Daughters of the American Revolution which does not, even today, permit any of the daughters of Crispus Attucks to join its ranks.

Not even the two Negro soldiers can presume that such a coterie has the interests of black people at heart. Such men and organizations offer evidence that America will, after this war is over, return once again to repressing Black people, rerunning the old film through the same old cameras, performing as the American people have always performed in the aftermath of every war in which Blacks have participated. The only difference this time will be that black people will no longer passively and quiescently accept such oppression.

There comes a time in the life of a people, as in the life of an individual, when each says to the oppressor, "No more, you have gone far enough." That moment has now arrived for black people. Young, articulate black men, who are refusing to serve in the war in Vietnam, are the inheritors of an experience which Crispus Attucks did not possess. They know that America is a racist society and that the fight for liberty and freedom must begin here where liberty and freedom are so blatantly denied, and that it affords a man nothing to make another country safe for democracy only to live under totalitarianism in his own.

But also, these men have no illusions. They know that America will continue to listen to the self-appointed guardians of her conscience—those Negroes who pass their own truths off as the truths of twenty million people. They know also, as certainly the Greek theatergoers must have known, that the *deus ex machina*, is little more than a mechanical construction, not the voice of man, but the instrument of man; holding out the hope of salvation which no honest men would dare to vouchsafe.

And they know, too, that even as the *deus ex machina* is wheeled into the living rooms of America—whether from the nation's capital in Ivy League suits, or from the battlefields of Vietnam in khaki brown and war gear—in an attempt to comfort white America, an increasing number of black men in the ghettos are refusing to join this war, refusing to once again become the laughing stock of history—fighting for a freedom which they themselves have never possessed—and refusing to allow the nonsensical rhetoric and empty phraseology of the machine gods to drown out their short, eloquent statement, "Hell no, Black men won't go!"

10

RACISM AND

THE AMERICAN UNIVERSITY

NOT SINCE THE EIGHTEENTH CENTURY has the American university been embroiled in more conflict than at present. In 1750 the conflict centered around control; would the university continue to be dominated by church denominations or would control pass to the states? In the famous Dartmouth College case of 1819 in which Daniel Webster appeared as attorney, the ruling of the court established the right of private, sectarian universities to exist free of state control. "The way was therefore open," notes Russell Blaine Nye in *The Cultural Life of the New Nation*, "for public and private institutions of higher education to develop separately, with the victory to the most powerful. In the ensuing struggle for educational dominance of the United States the religious institutions had by far the heavier guns."

The control of American higher education by religious denominations lasted until the middle of the nineteenth century. American colleges were little more than satellites of the Presbyterians, Methodists, and Baptists. They existed primarily to inculcate morals, dispense ethical values and propagandize on behalf of God and nation. Disdaining the plight of the poor, they were primarily concerned with the sons of the wealthy whom they attempted to provide with "a body of knowledge that would assure them of entrance into a community of educated leaders." In *Political Inquiries*, written in 1791, Robert Coram voiced objections to

99

this policy: "Education must not be . . . confined to the children of wealthy citizens; it is a shame, a scandal to civilized society, that part only of the citizens should be sent to colleges and universities."

Church domination of the institutions of higher learning meant that the university would be non-secular in mood as well as control. Ostensibly modeled after the universities of Europe— more specifically those of England—the early institutions did not encourage an atmosphere conducive to the free exchange of ideas. In a series of lectures given in 1852, John Henry, Cardinal, Newman, proposed the basis for such an atmosphere; but these were found irrelevent in a society which did not believe, with the Cardinal, that knowledge, "considered in a religious aspect, concurs with Christianity a certain way, and then diverges from it; and proves in the event, sometimes its serviceable ally, sometimes, from its very resemblance to it, an insidious and dangerous foe."

The church leaders considered knowledge unrelated to Christianity "a dangerous foe," and they kept a tight rein on college curricula. Their autocratic control led to serious controversy. "The first revolt against the traditional curriculum began in the middle of the eighteenth century. Expanding horizons in both scientific and non-scientific knowledge called for a broader collegiate education for broader purposes. American colleges had failed to reflect the changing character of American life. . . ."

The failure "to reflect the changing character of American life" is a censure under which the twentieth century university still labors. The blame does not lie with the university alone. In the latter part of the eighteenth century it reacted to intense pressure, not from students, but rather from the church fathers, politicians and wealthy citizens. Each of these factions wanted the university to cater to their interests, thus necessitating certain changes in the curricula. The church demanded a continuation of moral and ethical training; therefore its members sought retention of curricula embodying moralistic themes. The politicians, acting out of a sense of nationalism, demanded a shift from the preoccupation with morals and ethics to the inculcation of ideals of patriotism. The importance of science and technology to the business world caused men of wealth to demand a curriculum more favorably disposed to these disciplines. The university, which had traditionally reacted more favorably to the demands of outside special interest groups than it had to those of its own students, complied with all three demands. Thus, the curriculum of the nineteenth century university differed radically from that of previous centuries.

For the university, the consequences were grave. In conforming to the wishes of special interest groups outside its structure, it surrendered all possibility of existing as an independent institution devoted to the pursuit of knowledge. During the nineteenth century, it became the pawn of forces far more dangerously sectarian than the most dogmatic religious order. In the southern states, the policy which determined the content of the curriculum was dictated by politicians. In other parts of the country, the institutions came under the dictatorship of wealthy alumni whose control was often as tyrannical as that of the southern politicians.

By the end of the nineteenth century, the university had ceased its attempt to become an independent agency for the dissemination of creative, independent thought. Outwardly it maintained its appearance of a cloistered monastery where wise monks, devoted to the pursuit of wisdom, discoursed with eager, inquisitive students. However, in reality, the university was the home of men whose political and religious attitudes were merely replicas of those in the world outside. The appraisal of American universities as liberal institutions remains one of the purest examples of the elasticity of the English language.

Far from being liberal, the universities have been the most conservative, reactionary and racist institutions in the American society. Like the tides, they demonstrate the remarkable ability to move back and forth with the varying times. After the Civil War, when the conservative movement dominated America politically, economically and socially, the trend of the university was toward conservatism. When Franklin D. Roosevelt's New Deal policies produced a new wave of liberalism, it executed an almost one hundred and eighty degree turn to the left. In only one area has the university maintained equilibrium throughout its history—the area of race relations.

There was no necessity to institute change in this area. The policies of the nation concerning black people have changed little since the days of Reconstruction. No special interest group pressured the university to change policy or curricula in deference to Blacks. The "responsible" Negro leaders and their organizations, whose memberships usually include a large number of college professors, waged their war against state governments, primarily in the South, and ignored the university. Always few in number, black college professors found themselves (those who made the attempt) unable to effect change.

Dr. DuBois who attempted to institute the first Black Studies program in America, although he did not call it by that name, was stymied in his efforts by a conservative faction in American education led by Booker T. Washington. Washington, who had long been the darling of the educational establishment, supplied, through his philosophy and work at Tuskegee Institute, the rationale which enabled the university to continue along its well established route. Long before Washington enunciated his educational formula for the Negro in "The Atlanta Exposition Address," the men who controlled the institutions of higher education had put the theory into practice.

Washington was not an independent thinker. The policy he advocated and the formula he followed had been developed by General Armstrong at Hampton Institute. As a student at Hampton, Washington carefully observed the effect of industrial education upon black and Indian students. He concluded that the Indians did not possess the capacity to learn technical skills, whereas Blacks showed great proficiency. No intellectual, having reached this conclusion and armed with a personal disdain for creative thought, he began to dream of a black university in which the "practical and useful arts were to be taught."

The business and educational establishments were willing to help him realize his dream. They founded normal schools in the South and community colleges in the North. The aims of both institutions were similar: train Blacks to be the servants and lackeys of white America. In the South this meant education designed to produce carpenters, maids, agricultural workers and petty businessmen; in the North, to produce nurse's aides, orderlies, clerical helpers and lab technicians.

In addition, conforming to the ideals prevalent in the society outside its walls, the men from the universities developed not only the theories to justify their proposed educational program for Blacks, but also the theories which tended to validate the black man's inferiority. A summary of the many arguments from university professors, North and South, was supplied by the educator, Thomas Pearce Bailey in 1913. Bailey wrote: "The white race must dominate. The Teutonic peoples stand for race purity. The Negro is inferior and will remain so. This is a white man's country. No social equality. No political equality. In matters of civil rights and legal adjustments give the white man, as opposed to the colored man, the benefit of the doubt; and under no circumstances interfere with the prestige of the white race. In educational policy let the Negro have the crumbs that fall from the white man's table. Let there be such industrial education of the Negro as will best fit him to serve the white man. The status of peasantry is all the Negro may hope for, if the races are to live in peace. Let the lowest white man count for more than the highest Negro. The above statements indicate the leadings of providence."

To say that Bailey reflected the attitude of every college educator in America would be a gross distortion. To say that his opinions were held by a large number then and now is not. There have always been conscientious, dedicated men in the universities intent on moving it toward the fulfillment of its function of independent, creative education. Their attempts have been stifled, their idealism dissipated through their inability to deal with the Baileys who have the support of powerful interest groups both in and out of the university. Men who hold Bailey's sentiments wield power in many universities and, although their language differs from that of the former educator (the City College of New York is an exception; there, the Baileys have not been reluctant to declaim in the language and tone of their predecessor), their aims remain the same. Furthermore, riding a wave of conservative reactionism, today they are in a position to fulfill their aims.

The student rebellions of the past few years have been ineffective because the rebels have not realized this fact. Those who sought to change the university, black and white, neglected to do their homework. They chose targets of little real substance. The college administrator no longer exercises power as he did in the seventeenth and eighteenth centuries. At that time, his word was law. He could dismiss instructors and students with impunity; he could set arbitrary standards and demand that they be adhered to; his was the final word on curriculum. He answered only to the church authorities who were usually in complete accord.

When the universities came under more ruthless secular control in the nineteenth century, the erosion of the administrator's power began. This change was completed by the institution of the tenure system which allowed a group of individuals, reflecting the conservative nature of the society, to seize and maintain power. The result has been that, in the twentieth century, college presidencies have become ceremonial, not policy making positions, and the occupants of these positions have no more power than the students.

Real power resides in the hands of the faculty. It is they who set policy, determine curriculum content and develop admission requirements. More often than not, they run the university in a manner more dictatorial and capricious than the early church fathers would have thought possible. They are men of limited vision and questionable capacity whose ideas of education belong to the age of Aquinas and the Scholastics. They are young and old, black and white, and their most suitable metaphor is Dr. Bledsoe, the college president in Ralph Ellison's *Invisible Man*.

The controversy in higher education in the twentieth century centers about the arrogant use of faculty power to impede change and maintain the *status quo* in the political, economic and social areas of American life. This arrogant use of power, exercised in the interests of racism and reactionism, is, at present, nowhere exhibited more blatantly than at the City College of the City University of New York.

C.C.N.Y. has been designated—erroneously to be sure—as "a great liberal institution." This was due in part to the policy of the college, enacted at its inception, of enrolling the children of white minority groups. At the same time and ever since, it has practically closed its doors to the children of the black and Puerto

Rican minorities who live in the neighborhoods surrounding its Gothic buildings. The greatest enrollment of black students in the college's history occurred in 1965, and the manner in which this token enrollment was effected evidences the power and racism of the faculty.

Despite the fact that Dr. Kenneth Clark, the well known psychologist and advocate of integration, has occupied a prominent position on the faculty of the college for close to ten years, the initial impetus to enroll more black and Puerto Rican students came, not from the apostle of integration but from two white men, Bernard Levy and Leslie Berger. With little encouragement from Dr. Clark and no help, the two educators conceived the Pre-Baccalaureate Program. The program, to paraphrase Berger, was designed to offer minority students from New York City's ghetto areas an opportunity for a college education.

The program was begun during the summer when the majority of the senior faculty was on vacation. When the faculty returned to find the program in operation, in the fall of 1965, they began to develop stratagems to limit its effectiveness. Later, when the Pre-Bac Program became the model for the S.E.E.K. (Search for Educational Excellence through Knowledge) Program, the opposition increased. The threat of even greater numbers of Blacks and Puerto Ricans brought forth new stratagems, this time designed to destroy the program.

The proposals ranged from creation of a new community college in Harlem to which the students could be transferred, to the purchase of the Music and Art High School for the incarceration of the S.E.E.K. staff and student body. Another proposal was to keep the students on campus but to give them special courses for the entire four years, at the completion of which they would receive special degrees. The most effective plan was developed under the auspices of the English Department. Of all the departments, the English Department faced a special dilemma. It had opposed the Vietnam war and gained a reputation—in matters which did not pertain to Blacks—of being liberal. To have rejected the students outright would have been to reveal the racism which the members had assured themselves they did not possess.

To have accepted the students into the educational life of the department would have forced the members to reveal their own deficiencies in educational skills and techniques.

The English Department moved in the direction which has been sanctioned ever since by departments and colleges searching for ways to minimize contact between whites and Blacks in an educational setting. It created a special branch of the department and hired a special staff of black teachers. It attempted to discourage white teachers who applied to teach in the program and offered them positions in the regular department instead. It frowned upon those of its own members who were committed to true education and demanded to teach S.E.E.K. students. Therefore, within the English Department there existed a separate program with a staff and student body composed primarily of Blacks and Puerto Ricans. Dr. Clark, who resigned from the board of Antioch College due to an allegedly similar situation, retains his position on the faculty of C.C.N.Y.

During the uprising of 1969, black and Puerto Rican members of the Student Coalition put forth as one of their five demands a greater voice in controlling the program. What they sought was the validation of the policy already being practiced by the English Department. Since the program was separate in every aspect except control, why not also relinquish this to Blacks and Puerto Ricans? In other words, extending the formula enacted by the English Department, why should a program primarily designed for Blacks and Puerto Ricans which had been effectively transformed into a segregated program, not go all the way and become separate in every essential? The faculty balked. To maintain a separate program was one thing; to allow Blacks and Puerto Ricans to control it was another. However, with the exception of the question of control, the students and the faculty, to paraphrase William Blake, were both of the same devilish party without even knowing it.

What began as an attempt to legalize existing policy, quickly degenerated into a conflict between black and white. Black and Puerto Rican faculty and students became the objects of the type of verbal abuse which does honor to the memory of Senator Vardaman of Mississippi, who took great pride in his extensive vocabulary of racial epithets. Students were called "animals" and "misfits," faculty members were called "boys," "girls" and "niggers." The epithets were hurled by faculty members from the floor and rostrum during faculty meetings attended by black and white students. Once, in my presence, the newly elected Acting President, Joseph Copeland, referred to white students who supported the goals of the Blacks as "white trash."

Racist attitudes which had heretofore been visible only to individual black and Puerto Rican students in classrooms, when papers were returned or their examinations marked, flared into the open as the faculty could no longer restrain itself. Much of it, to be sure, was occasioned by the student seizure of the south campus. But, this act alone does not suffice as an explanation of the terrible spectacle presented by college teachers shouting epithets at black students, encouraging white students to display Nazi insignia, and performing with an hysteria and paranoia whose closest analogue is to be found in the lynch mobs, legendary in American history. The frenzied actions of the faculty mob were motivated by more threatening forces than the student occupation of buildings.

At the close of the Fall semester of 1968, prior to the student revolt, the English Department hired Dr. Wilfred Cartey, the distinguished, internationally known scholar of Black history and culture, to institute a Black Studies Program. (During the turmoil when Professor Cartey was charged with being a tool of the Black Panther Party and having been brought to the college by this organization, the English Department did not attempt to clarify the issue or to refute the charges—the reason is clear: by that time, the English Department had had second thoughts about its choice.) Cartey was a scholar first; and with the keen analytical mind of the scholar, he divined the forces at work on the campus. They were the same forces that were at work on campuses throughout the nation. The rash of instant Black Studies Programs, ill-equipped, poorly organized and inadequately staffed, is merely a ploy of contemporary racists to perpetuate the miseducation of black students, a policy which has been the hallmark of the American university.

Few of these programs are worth the paper they are drawn

on. Designed to benefit neither black nor white students, their objectives are to remove the burden of educational responsibility from the shoulders of the older, tenured faculty. To be effective, a Black Studies Program must be interdisciplinary. It must effect change in every liberal arts department in the university. In so doing, far from being, as Bayard Rustin insists, a cathartic exercise for black students, such a program would radicalize the university and transform it into a truly educational institution.

To understand this statement, one must first be aware of the inadequacy of existing college curricula: In history courses on both the undergraduate and graduate levels, the contributions of Frederick Douglass, David Walker, Henry Highland Garnet and Booker T. Washington to the making of the American nation are deleted; neither Phillis Wheatley, Paul Laurence Dunbar, Claude McKay nor Langston Hughes are read or studied in English courses. Students of sociology are not required to read DuBois, E. Franklin Frazier, Weaver or Kenneth Clark. The same omissions are repeated in political science, music and economics.

A realistic Black Studies Program would therefore force such delinquent departments to restructure their courses to include the contributions of minority groups. Far from being an isolated, segregated enclave existing somewhere in the hinterlands of the campus, the Black Studies Department would be a powerful institution capable of producing a renaissance in American thought and education.

Fred Cartey entertained such ideas. For this reason, he found himself caught between the Black and Puerto Rican student and faculty community and the white faculty. To once more paraphrase William Blake, the antagonists were working in the interests of the same deity. With few exceptions, neither the black students nor faculty had the least idea of what a program of Black and Puerto Rican Studies entailed. In lieu of understanding they substituted emotionalism which often took the form of demands for the improbable, incapable of being fulfilled by anyone who did not have the power of Zeus, the wisdom of Apollo and the patience of Job. They knew that they had been cheated out of their cultural heritage. But, they did not know how to force the university to make amends.

On the other hand, the white faculty, old hands at deceiving black students, knew what kind of Black Studies Program they would allow from the very beginning. Like the Pre-Bac Program, they wanted it to be separate. The teaching of black history and literature in a separate institution, run by Blacks for Blacks, would lessen the pressure on the senior faculty members. Veterans of the white liberal tradition, having marched to Washington with Martin Luther King and attended meetings of the N.A.A.C.P., they knew how to mesmerize the natives by presenting the appearance of action without committing substantive acts.

Dr. Cartey's proposal called for the creation of a School of Black and Puerto Rican Studies whose far reaching effects would go beyond changing the traditional departmental curricula. More important, the program called for extensive exploration and study of areas of interest, not only to the student body, but also to the black and Puerto Rican community outside the college. From the moment that such a program, designed to bring large numbers of Blacks and Puerto Ricans together in an educational setting to study not only their own history and culture but that of the oppressor as well, was unveiled, Cartey's days at C.C.N.Y. were numbered. The Black and Puerto Rican Faculty-Student Coalition and their white supporters whose impotence was displayed at each faculty meeting, found themselves with no program at all. In the absence of any restraining power, the new president, acting in behalf, if not with the full knowledge, of his reactionary faculty, arbitrarily dismissed Dr. Cartey; and, functioning as the hachetman of the extremist faction, launched a verbal attack upon the scholar in the language fashionable among bigots from Mississippi to New York City.

The lesson to be learned from the C.C.N.Y. experience is important to students across the nation. The men who run America's educational establishment cover the spectrum from idealists to demogogues. At present, the political climate in America favors the demogogues. The special interest groups which influence educational policy from California to New York are dedicated to the proposition that the university will not change in any significant way. They are prepared only to offer palliatives instead of cures for the serious problems of the twentieth century.

Those most affected by this attitude are non-white minorities for whom the university has long been regarded as a stepping stone to success. They have watched colleges educate and prepare members of other minority groups to assume positions of importance in their communities. Three times within its history, City College lowered its standards in order to enable members of white minority groups to enroll. Today, many members of those groups support the faculty's attempt to keep black and Puerto Rican enrollment at a minimum. In addition, they constitute the special interest groups behind the politicians and college officials whose objective is to keep minority students within the limits of the Booker T. Washington formula.

They mask their racist attitudes behind seemingly legitimate reasons. The turn to repression and reaction on the campus, goes the rationale, is due to the student rebellions of the past few years. Most of these rebellions have been led and precipitated by white students; yet those who receive the brunt of the pressure are black. This pressure was intensified when a group of black students at Cornell University armed for self-protection after a fiery cross—the symbol of American tyranny which burns deep in the heart of every black man—was placed in front of the black women's dormitory. Denunciations came from Congress, the press and the more overt Negro haters across the country. The aim has been to depict black students as disrupters of the peaceful university which existed, in the words of a white South Carolinian, "before they removed God from the schools and let the niggers in."

The peaceful university has never existed. As Nye notes, ". . . the history of almost any nineteenth century college shows at least one serious outbreak. In 1807, 125 of Princeton's total enrollment of 200 were expelled for rioting. Harvard freshmen and sophomores in 1817 smashed all the college crockery; that same year Princeton students broke the dormitory windows and threw wine bottles and firewood at the faculty. At Hobart students rolled red-hot cannonballs down a dormitory corridor and seriously injured a faculty member. At North Carolina students shot out windows with guns, and at Virginia, the high-spirited Southern boys horsewhipped several faculty members. In 1814 Princeton students constructed a giant firecracker with a hollow log and two pounds of gunpowder and nearly blew up Nassau Hall. The class of 1824, in preparation for graduation at Dartmouth, 'burnt one barn, stoned Professor Chamberlain, burnt him and tutor Parley and hung the President in effigy.' Three Bowdoin students were expelled and a score of others disciplined in 1827 for setting off powder charges under tutors' chairs."

Neither the university community nor the community at large responded with repressive measures. Unlike his counterpart in New York City today, the President of Hobart College did not threaten the students with the Army, Navy and Marines. They were white students; therefore they were not placed in isolation, declared unworthy of an education, nor harassed by faculty members and fellow students. With far more limited resources than the college of today, the earlier institution moved to correct the problems which produced the disturbances.

That the same action will take place in the reactionary atmosphere of the present is doubtful. Having proven that it is merely one more racist institution in the society, the university seems determined to continue those policies which can only hasten the coming of what James Baldwin has described as "the fire next time."

In 1965, in a moment of unfounded optimism, in an article in the *Journal of Human Relations*, I described the new black and Puerto Rican students who had just entered City College in the following terms: "These young men and women are engaged in the process of ridding the American society of knot holes, of throwing open the doors of the world of intellect, of understanding through learning, scholarship and perseverance, not for themselves alone, but for all of those in this country, black and white, who comprise that segment of humanity which Franz Fanon has called 'the wretched of the earth.' " I was correct about the students. I was wrong about the university. The metaphor of the twentieth century is a university impervious to change and, unlike its predecessors of the middle ages, incapable of bringing order out of chaos and establishing the rule of reason. Had I been more perceptive in 1965, I would have advised my students in the words which Matthew Arnold used to advise a college dropout in "The Scholar Gypsy":

> Fly our paths, our feverish contact fly!
> For strong the infection of our mental strife
> Which, though it gives no bliss, yet spoils for rest;
> And we should win thee from thy own fair life,
> Like us distracted, and like us unblest.
> Soon, soon thy cheer would die.
> Thy hopes grow timorous, and unfixed thy powers
> And thy clear aims be cross and shifting made:
> And then thy glad perennial youth would fade
> Fade, and grow old at last, and die like ours.

11

THE EXPATRIATE

THE PILOT OF the TWA jetliner concluded his remarks: "Our flying time will be seven hours. We should reach New York at 8 P.M. Eastern Standard Time. We hope you enjoy your trip." The voice faded away. Passengers began to stir in their seats, looking at each other with compassion. Strange bedfellows are created ten thousand feet above the earth. Besides me, there were three other black passengers on the plane; two were women. One wore a blonde wig which hung down around her shoulders. She was, I suppose, a beautiful woman, yet her face had been made hideous by the mascara—undoubtedly purchased in a French shop— which she had applied too liberally. Almost as soon as the pilot had concluded his greeting, she struck up a conversation with the middle-aged white woman in the seat beside her. The other woman sat three rows in front of me. She wore blue slacks and a tight fitting blouse. As she leaned over to tap the shoulder of the white man sitting next to her, a gold medallion fell across her chest. Like the other, she too was soon engaged in a heated conversation. The other black passenger was a man, tall with thinning brown hair. He was seated next to a brunette who was listening to him with a courtesy that would have seemed unusual in the America to which we were all heading. There seemed to be little difference between one white passenger and another. They were, I supposed, middle-class Americans, the kind for whom reactionary

113

American politicians have recently begun to exude sympathy.

In Paris, they would have been found in the section which the French contemptuously refer to as the "American Compound." They were businessmen from Ohio, college students from Radcliffe, and honeymooners from Minnesota. They were true representatives of the American people: those who think, as James Baldwin has noted, that they own half the world. He might have added that they also act the part. Coming from a nation of conquerors, wherever they go—Italy, Germany, France, Spain—they exhibit the arrogance, condescension and bad manners of conquerors. They have become accustomed to regarding people in their native land who are different from them as inferiors; and this habit, nurtured and cultivated in the United States, causes them to project their Americanism upon all strangers so that each one becomes some form of nigger to them.

I had managed to avoid them in Europe. Now, ten thousand feet in the air, we were neighbors. Modern technology had brought us together and made comrades of us. We were bound to each other in a manner that I have never wanted to be bound to white people. No one boards an airplane expecting disaster, yet everyone realizes that disaster is always a possibility. The threat of death, although casually dismissed by each passenger, still hangs over everything like an invisible mist. The knowledge that one might die so instantaneously, without warning, prompts strangers who have never seen each other before, and who will never see each other again, to converse as if they were life-long friends. More remarkable, Blacks and whites are forced together in a bond of brotherhood inconceivable under any circumstance in America.

I noticed that the Americans appeared less American than before. The threat of death tempered their arrogance. The fire of contempt, so omnipresent in their eyes, the scowl, seemingly so permanently fixed upon their faces, had disappeared. They appeared almost human, and watching them—had one not known what they were like before and what they would quickly revert to once they had reached the earth—it was almost possible to feel sorry for them. They were in a position which was strange to them, one to which they were unaccustomed. If danger came, they had none of the usual advantages. They could not rely on their whiteness, their God, or their nationality; they would have to rely upon luck, and luck is an international, interracial phenomenon.

Out of a sense of dread, they extended the hand of compassion to those of us to whom before they had extended only the closed fist. They were so afraid to die that they struck me as being obscene. They were not anxious to meet that God whom they had palmed off on half of the world; they did not believe with Augustine that man lived to die so that he might have life everlasting. They did not wish to enter that eternal void where all sound is muted, where all vision is dimmed. Agents of their government were, at that very moment, dispensing death to millions in Vietnam in their name while they, fresh from their orgiastic feasting and dining in another land, sat like cringing animals. Suddenly I found myself muttering to the unhearing aircraft: "Plunge, plunge down through the morning haze, down through the golden rays of sunlight; plunge towards the carpet-like patches of land below, plunge us all into blackness, into nothingness, into eternity."

"Good to be going home again, hunh?" The voice frightened me back to reality. It belonged to the passenger on my left, who had been tossing in his seat, attempting to read *Time Magazine*, but unable to keep his eyes off of the window. We had boarded the plane almost at the same moment. But not until now had he attempted to converse with me. "No!" I replied brusquely. He frowned. The arrogance, mingled with contempt, came back to his face. He hunched his shoulders, reached into his vest pocket for a cigar, and defiantly turned his back to me. I smiled. "Going home!" He had meant it as a courtesy. He had no way of knowing what the words meant to me. On the other hand, I had no way of telling him other than the brusque, defiant, "No!"

The stewardess appeared at my elbow. I ordered a drink and settled back in my seat. On my lap, the sensitive face of James Baldwin peered up from the jacket of *The Fire Next Time*. I remembered that the French held him in high esteem despite the shockingly true statements that he had made about their country. He was studied at the Sorbonne with a reverence that American academicians pay only to Tolstoy, Eliot and Joyce. No French-man whom I had ever met had complained about the "looseness of his novels, the improbability of his characters"; none argued that he should write essays instead of novels. They only wanted him to continue writing.

What they liked most about him, I suppose, was his honesty. And it was this which Americans most disliked about him. In his essays, he has set down the details of his life with an objectivity and openness displayed by no other writer since Thomas De Quincey. Yet, primarily because of so doing, he has been labelled subversive by his countrymen. Not only whites—who label all opponents subversive—have so labelled him, but also Blacks who should know better. He is America's modern-day Socrates, and like the Socrates of old, his dose of hemlock has been prepared and administered with the disdain that nations and individuals alike have accorded their prophets throughout recorded history.

Sometime ago he found life in America unbearable. He left the land of his birth, travelled to Paris, and succeeded in creating a new life. The Baldwin who left America to return no more differs greatly from the Baldwin who periodically returns as an internationally famous writer. However, it is the first Baldwin who captured the imagination of the world, and nothing was more instrumental in aiding in that capture than the essay, "Notes of a Native Son," in the book by that title. The first half of the essay deals with the circumstances which eventually propelled Baldwin to Paris. In brilliant lines reminiscent of DuBois, he describes the cataclysmic experience he underwent in a New Jersey restaurant.

After waiting for an intolerably long time, the waitress finally approached his table, hesitantly pronouncing the words, "We don't serve Negroes here . . . I pretended not to have under-stood her," wrote Baldwin, "hoping to draw her closer. And she did step a very short step closer, with her pencil poised incongru-ously over her pad, and repeated the formula: '. . . don't serve Negroes here.'

"Somehow, with the repetition of that phrase, which was already ringing in my head like a thousand bells of a nightmare, I realized that she would never come any closer and that I would have to strike from a distance. There was nothing on the table but an ordinary water-mug half full of water, and I picked this up and hurled it with all my strength at her. She ducked and it missed her and shattered against the mirror behind the bar. And, with that sound, my frozen blood abruptly thawed, I returned from wherever I had been, I *saw* for the first time, the restaurant, the people with their mouths open, already, as it seemed to me, rising as one man, and I realized what I had done, and where I was, and I was frightened. I rose and began running for the door. A round, potbellied man grabbed me by the nape of my neck just as I reached the doors and began to beat me about the face. I kicked him and got loose and ran into the streets."

After this harrying experience, having escaped from the insane mob which pursued him, Baldwin related, "I could not get over two facts, both equally difficult for the imagination to grasp, and one was that I could have been murdered. But the other was that I had been ready to commit murder."

"Ready to commit murder." The plane struck an airpocket, lurched to the right and straightened up again. I ordered another drink. Baldwin's words floated around in my skull. They were similar to other words, more recent, more personal words which had lodged in my mind and occupied, so it seems, a permanent place there. These words had also come from an exile—a more permanent one than Baldwin had proven to be—who had taken up residence in Paris and attempted to create a new life for himself, as I had done. We had been friends before, very close friends, and it was out of respect for that one-time friendship that he told me, in words as eloquent as those of Baldwin: "I had to leave that damn place. I mean, I had to leave, otherwise I would have killed myself."

We stood in Paris on the Right Bank. Behind us was the Louvre, directly below, between the parapet and the water, was a narrow road which French motorists used as a freeway. In the distance, the Eiffel Tower stood like an Egyptian princess, vying with the golden stars for majesty and glory. The waters of the

Seine were peaceful and calm, stirred only by the double-deckered *bateaux-mouches* loaded with Germans, Spaniards and Americans.

In 1958, shortly after graduating from college, Roland set sail for Europe. He left America hurriedly, without stopping to visit his family in North Carolina or to say goodby to those of us who loved him. When we discovered that he was gone, we searched his favorite haunts in New York and, failing to find him, concluded that he had returned South. No one considered the possibility that he had left America forever, that he had chosen to seek refuge in a saner, more rational land.

Roland was not a famous personality; he was neither an intellectual nor an idealist. He was a hard worker, the plodding kind who stuck to a task until he completed it. Moreover, he was a country boy who had learned to live, love and laugh while helping his family attempt to eke a living out of the tough Carolina soil. "My mother wants me to be a preacher," he once confided to me. His bright eyes flashing, he added, "she wants to protect me." He did not want to be protected. He only wanted to be left alone; he wanted to live a life free of insult; he wanted to sleep at night unconcerned about the experiences that tomorrow would bring. He wanted to live a life in which no one was free to challenge his dignity or to threaten his self-respect. "I don't want to tear down this country," he said, "I don't want to save it. All I want is for white people to leave me alone."

Three months after he arrived in Paris, I received his first and only letter. He wrote of his life in Paris, of his attempt to find work, of the African girl he had met at the Sorbonne. He concluded the letter: ". . . and you know, the French don't bother me, don't get into my hair. Not because they're so damn moral. But you see, they have their niggers in the Algerians; so they don't annoy me." But much later I learned that he had undergone an American experience in Paris.

The incident occurred in Chartres, where Roland had spent the night with a friend. While waiting for the train to take him back to Paris, he had stopped off at a restaurant. He was carrying a small suitcase which he placed beside his chair. The waitress, nonchalantly balancing a tray containing three mugs of coffee, tripped over the bag, dashing the coffee to the floor. She recovered quickly, placed her hands on her hips, and shouted at him in broken English, "You dam neegar." "I had not heard those words addressed to me in such a long time," he confided, "that I turned around to see if perhaps she was speaking to someone else. When the full effect of what she said hit me, I laughed. She looked so funny, you know, she looked so funny—like she had just learned the words."

There was no laughter now. I had met him at a bad time. He had lost his job as an interpreter for a foreign newspaper. He was forced to live off of the earnings of his wife. My appearance at this time of desperation served only to remind him of all that he had tried so hard to forget. Although we had been the best of friends, I was now an American to him; and though he was too kind to admit it, I symbolized all that had previously disgusted him, all that had caused him pain. My presence conjured up for him the same anguish and dread that white people have ofttimes conjured up for me.

"I have not loved the world, nor the world me," wrote Lord Byron, "but let us part fair foes. . . ." Roland would settle for no such pact. Between him and America there was a vendetta and no expanse of water and land could lessen the enmity which he bore her. The country which had given him birth, which had nursed him, had proceeded to betray him in every conceivable way, had even, as Baldwin notes, set him down in the ghetto to die. It had succeeded in creating an implacable foe whose hatred became so overwhelming that, for the sake of self-preservation, he was forced to desert his family, friends and career.

I recalled Boris Pasternak's words: "Every mother gives birth to a genius. It is not her fault that somewhere along the way something goes wrong." Everything went wrong for Roland. He lived in America for thirty-three years and he suffered the constant day-to-day erosion of his manhood as he attempted to thwart the purposive, determined effort of every American institution to subdue him, to break his spirit, to convince him that he was little more than a subhuman animal—"the bastard child of humanity."

Almost from the time of his birth, his country declared war

on him and waged it ferociously. He had not wanted this war. He was a man of peace. Nevertheless, he soon learned that to be Black in America is to be constantly at war with society and, despite his reluctance, once he became engaged, he was determined to fight the war to its conclusion. Then the unexpected happened.

"I came home from work," he said. (He was the only Black in an integrated building in a Jewish neighborhood in the Bronx which was quickly changing its ethnic composition.) "There was this little girl. She always did the same thing. When she got on the elevator, if she saw me coming, she would wait until I got close and close the door. She saw her mother do it one day. I guess that's why she did it. This day, I didn't see her. When I reached the elevator, she began to pull the door. This time I was close enough to get my foot in. I pried it open." He paused. Over on the Left Bank some college students were making their nightly trip down the steps leading to the river bank, sleeping bags slung carelessly across their shoulders. Roland continued, "I walked inside and stood near her. But she wasn't scared. She moved over to the corner and stood there looking at me. She was only about eight years old, but she looked as arrogant as any cracker I've ever seen."

He had wanted to kill her. She was only a child and she was ignorant of the far reaching effects of her actions. She could not know what this childish act meant to a man whose life had been shaped in a country where even the most innocent prank takes on the grotesque appearance of the deadly serious. The American story is writ large in the antics of this child; and it is this complete and total disrespect for human dignity passed from old Americans to young, which occasions my loathing and disgust for this country. One can imagine what has happened to the child. She has probably gone off to college, graduated, married, and settled down in some white enclave in the suburbs enjoying a measure of happiness unknown to the majority of Americans. The recipient of her abuse, on the other hand, walks the narrow streets of Paris, a stranger in a strange land among strange people, trying to find work to enable him to keep his family from starving. The only happiness he knows, that he will ever know, is that he has prevented his child from being brought up in America.

"I wanted to kill her." he continued. "And then I knew that I couldn't do it. She was just a child. But then, you know, I realized how impotent I was." His voice broke. Perhaps he was crying; I do not know. I had turned my eyes toward the Eiffel Tower. "I realized that I could never take action against them unless I killed them. But I knew too that I couldn't kill—not unless it was myself. And if I had stayed there, after awhile, I would've killed myself."

Each day in America, especially since the summer disturbances, those Rolands who have chosen to remain are confronted by whites who ask their "overwhelming question." What they desire to know most of all is why many Blacks have stopped talking to them. We must communicate, they tell the black Rolands, continue to talk to one another. Their pleas fall on deaf ears. Like Roland, millions of his brothers refuse to hold dialogue with whites, refuse to attempt to "communicate" with them. The reason is not difficult to ascertain. Dialogue can take place only between equals and no white man is the equal of Roland. None can approach his level of pain and suffering, none can attain his position of awareness, and none can divest himself of his whiteness and enter that world where the tendency toward suicide is omnipresent. Roland lives in a world far outside the boundaries of sociologists, psychologists and pseudo-intellectuals.

In that world, somewhere in a past almost too painful to recall, a child humiliated him. In so doing, she symbolized his helplessness against all he would confront for the rest of his life. Awareness came, sudden but not dramatic, shorn of color and spectacle. It was heralded by no miraculous event. There was no lynching of a loved one, no beating—although he had once been beaten by racist New York City policemen. The vehicle of the awakening was the inheritor of America's mores and values—a white child—insensitive, not capable of realizing the terrible toll she was exacting from another human being.

The stewardess appeared with a tray. I checked my watch. In four hours I would once again be on American soil. I released the folded table from the back of the seat in front of me, waited while the stewardess set my tray down and began to dab at my food. Throughout our conversation, Roland continued, with obvious cynicism, to use the phrase, "your country," when speaking about America. It was as if he had given away an unwanted gift and couldn't refrain from deriding the new recipient for accepting it. I recalled the words and smiled. Once, another expatriate, more famous than Roland would ever be, had become incensed by white men who insisted that America was their country. One can imagine an enraged DuBois assaulting blank sheets of paper, throwing words on them with the fury of a Pollock flinging paint upon a canvas.

"Your country!" the old warrior had written in his youth, "How came it yours? Before the pilgrims landed we were here. Here we brought our three gifts and mingled them with yours: a gift of story and song—soft stirring melodies in an ill harmonized and unmelodious land—the gift of sweat and brawn to beat back the wilderness, conquer the soil, and lay the foundations of this vast economic empire two hundred years earlier than your weak hands could have done it; the third, a gift of the spirit—our song, our cheer, and warning have been given to this nation in blood-brotherhood. Are not these gifts worth giving? Is not this work and striving? Would America have been America without her Negro people?"

One wonders at what point the sage first damned himself and his people for offering such gifts to so undeserving a nation. When did he conclude that those who laid claim to America had the power to substantiate their claims, thus negating any question of ownership? At what point did he realize with Richard Wright, another famous black expatriate, that ". . . America's barbaric treatment of the Negro was not one-half so bad as the destructive war which she waged, in striking at the Negro, against the concept of the free person, against freedom of conscience, against the rights of man, and against herself."

The answer has accompanied him to the grave. However, realization must have set in after he had been persecuted, harassed and ridiculed by the United States Government while the NAACP, that guardian of the black man's dignity, stood by in abject silence. When realization did occur, when he, like Roland, was impressed with his own helplessness, his own powerlessness, he too deserted the home of his father and surrendered to the American

Caesar the land which his power enabled him to claim as his own.

The realization that one has been betrayed by the land of his birth is a painful experience. At the outset, each man regards the country in which he is born as a special Eden, a utopia on earth. He is likely to grow up loving it, willing to lay down his life in defense of it. The country is analogous to a mother and he regards her as such, demanding the same tenderness, care and warmth. They are truly parent and child, and each has responsibilities to the other. The bond between them is as much a blood tie as that between mother and son for, unlike Faust, the citizen has not bargained away his soul to the country, but given it freely, without hesitation. Of no people in the world is this more true than of Blacks in America.

One takes the painful journey back into his own past, back to the time of innocence, to the time of "sweetness and light," to the time before pain is real enough to be felt, before fear has been shaped, to a time—so long ago—when hate, bitterness and animosity were words found only in the vocabularies of adults. There was the schoolhouse, a small, neat, three-story building made of red brick and named for John Marshall, a Supreme Court Justice. Each morning, before the lessons began, there were prayers, followed by pledges of allegiance to the flag. One flag was atop the blackboard. The other was outside, atop a large pole, fluttering in the morning breeze.

Like the others, I sat with my head bowed, though turned sideways so that I could focus my eyes on the more majestic flag outside. When we pledged allegiance, my heart tumbled with joy; a sensation of belonging to something good and wonderful came over me. At an early age I sensed the might and power of America, and I believed that I was a part of it. This belief brought tears to my eyes on many a morning. There was no outside world for me, no world of adults, no world of ugly things. America the beautiful and God, two inseparable beings whom I loved with the same tenderness as I felt for my mother and father.

I knew that my country was at war. In my hometown, men, dressed in crisp khaki, paraded through the streets. They were my heroes. I wanted to be like them, to wear the colors of my country, to fight my country's enemies. I knew that these enemies were called Japs and Germans. Once I accompanied a group of adults who invaded a restaurant, dragged a Japanese outside (it was later discovered that he was Chinese), beat him, and set fire to his place of business. I had taken no part in the action although I had sympathized with the mob. Not until much later did I realize why my father had beaten me for even being among the group; and not until later still was I to hate myself for displaying such chauvinism.

The love of America which blossomed during the years of innocence died soon after. Every institution outside of the ghetto in which I lived seemed determined to prove that I was merely a ward of the country and not an essential part of it. At first I was bewildered, then bewilderment turned to disbelief, until finally, incidents accumulated and disbelief turned to realization. From churches, schools, and economic institutions, the echo reverberated across the country assaulting my young mind, shattering the dream of a bond of love and unity between America and me. The words were written in the face of almost every white person I met and they were always the same: "This is the white man's country."

One day I no longer saw the flag. It had not been removed from the flagpole; it had been removed from my mind's eye. The words of the pledge of allegiance stuck in my throat. I refused to sing "The Star Spangled Banner" or "America, the Beautiful." I began to sympathize with the Japanese. I realized that the nation which had dropped the atomic bomb on their land, which had destroyed their children, was guilty of infanticide long before the atomic bomb was developed. That nation, to paraphrase William Faulkner, which sanctions the death of a young child, does not deserve to survive and probably will not.

"You're leaving tomorrow?" asked Roland, breaking a long silence. I replied somewhat hesitantly, "Yes, I'm going back to it; back to the sham, the hypocrisy, the place where they lie just for kicks." He smiled for the first time. A look of affection came into his eyes, then, just as suddenly, it disappeared. Once he had felt affection for me. Now I was suspect. Nothing that had transpired between America and me would be important to him until I had severed all connections with her, physical and mental. After awhile I added, "I have to go back."

He did not ask why. Perhaps he already knew. He knew that I had no illusions. I did not believe that America would ever become better. I did not believe that black people could be saved, and I did not believe that America was worth saving. I was tired of the daily warfare, had become numbed by the incessant friction and the physical—not to mention mental—effort necessary to survive for one week without going insane. Nevertheless, in a few hours I would be on a plane heading back to a land which I refused to acknowledge as my own.

I turned away from him. "There is," I said haltingly, addressing the words more to myself than to him, "a tragedy being played out in America. Whatever is good in America, whatever is important, is important because black people are there. The Americans have never been able to understand this and they never will. Many black men who feel as I do, will no longer try to tell them. We will tell the truth regardless of what it costs—but not for the benefit of the whites. We will tell the truth to black people. I go back to tell my truth."

On the plane a movie screen had been set up. The passenger in the seat next to me attached the ear plugs to the outlet in the seat arm. The steady stream of conversation lessened, and above the silence, the roar of the engines sounded like millions of honey bees. I checked my watch again. America lay two hours in the future. I ordered another drink.

"They will kill you." Roland had replied quickly. "If they don't, you'll go crazy. Nobody in America wants the truth. Whites don't want it; Blacks don't want it. They'll kill you."

"Yes," I replied, "truth is a dangerous thing in America, even a private truth. Even if you say that it's your own, that you don't offer it dogmatically, but only in the realm of free ideas. Yes, I know, but I must go back; and there is no other reason."

That was all we said. We lapsed into silence. After a short while, he gripped my hand, smiled, and left. I watched him cross the bridge which separated the Left Bank from the Right; his head held high, his stride more purposeful than it had been in America. Once on the other side, he paused to wave at me. Then he was gone, back to his apartment in the Algerian quarter, back to his African wife and child.

I remained, looking down into the crystal clear waters of the Seine. I remembered that here in this land to which so many black men had come to forget, Danton, a revolutionary sentenced to the guillotine by his comrade in arms, had remarked prophetically, "Robespierre will follow me." And I remembered too that tomorrow I would be back in America where I would have to readjust my whole life style, pay attention to insignificant acts of protocol which I had not needed during my stay in Paris, redevelop stratagems simply to stay alive. I could not help but wonder: "At what point would Roland become my Danton, and at what time in the future would I follow in his footsteps?"

12

DREAMS OF

A NATIVE SON

I WAS INTRODUCED TO the concept of the bogey man by my mother, a passionate believer in Christianity. Previously, she had attempted to discipline me by conjuring up images of the devil. When the attempt failed, she used her talent for metaphorical language and painted a frightening, vivid description of the bogey man. As she described him, he was ten times more vicious than the devil, five times more intent on devouring black children and, whereas the devil was ugly, the bogey man was hideous. He had red eyes and red hair, redder even than the coals of hell, and a grey, fishy skin which shone bright and garish when illuminated by the sunlight.

She had not intended to supply me with a racial image. Yet, nevertheless, when the bogey man took form in my mind, the form was that of a white man. This may have been because the only white man I knew, the insurance man, had red hair and red eyes. And though he was not an ugly man, my imagination supplied those characteristics to his features which transformed him into an ogre.

Sometime later, having been threatened with the bogey man for perhaps the fifteenth time, I confronted the ogre in a dream. Here his hair was redder than in waking life and his eyes protruded like long binoculars from both sides of his face. In one of his fishy, grey hands he carried a wide steel net which he threw over me again and again, as each time I miraculously made my escape. Finally he approached me with a net larger than any before, stalked me like a spider stalking its prey, and maneuvered me at last into a corner from which escape was impossible.

At this point I awoke in a cold sweat, and screamed into the darkness. "Don't let that white man get me! Momma, don't let that white man get me!" The dream has never recurred. And though I have often given much thought to it, I cannot begin to understand its meaning. One thing, however, seems clear: at the age of five, I was concerned about and frightened by the racial situation.

This is not surprising. By that time I had had my "Fire baptism" in the lava-hot waters of Southern racial prejudice. One day, while waiting for my mother in a department store, I stood against a table upon which various garments were arrayed. A white woman approached with a youngster not much older than myself. The young boy wandered over to the counter and, ignoring me, picked up a sweater and began to examine it. Suddenly, his mother, like an enraged, wounded beast, sprang to the counter, snatched the sweater from the child's hands, dropped it hastily upon the table, and pointed an accusing finger at me: "Can't you see that little nigger beside them clothes," she screeched; "he probably been trying 'em on too. You want to catch germs?"

Records of such incidents would easily fill a library shelf. The naive see them as trivial, simply minutiae relative to the lynchings and bombings which are a part of many Negroes' experiences. Others, have yet to learn what the average Black has always known; lynching is a word whose connotation cannot be restricted to assaults upon the body alone; brutal though such acts may be, the most vicious brutalization, the most terrible of all lynchings, are those which, in the long run, disfigure the mind.

For me, therefore, white people became natural symbols for things evil. And this symbolism manifested itself in the most trivial ways. Sitting on the backyard fence one Sunday morning, I watched two stray dogs in combat. One was almost pure black; the other dirty white. Neither dog was familiar; yet instinctively I sided with the black dog, egging him on with the epitaph: "Kill that dirty cracker!" I had no problem with identity.

Such incidents stand out in my mind, remembrances of things not really past but ominously ever-present, suggesting that for one Negro at least, to paraphrase Leopold Senghor, the past and the present must always be confused; and that not even in the unconscious can one be free of the realities of everyday life.

Yet the black unconscious, in the main, lies immune to exploration. Psychologists, sociologists, and anthropologists are more interested in exploring the similarities between black and white than in dealing with the universe of differences. Too often white and black psychologists attempt to apply the rules of the academy equally to black and white alike. As a psychologist, working in a college program with predominantly black students, confided to me; "Race may be the most important thing to these students, but I doubt it. I think that I can deal with them on the same grounds that I deal with other students . . . at least, I have to; these are the only grounds I know."

By other students I suppose he meant white students, and beyond them, white Americans in general. If so, the argument is not feasible. Black Americans cannot be "dealt with" like white Americans, for despite the argument of the assimilationists, Black Americans are different from white Americans. In many subconscious utterances, black people acknowledge this fact. Recently, a "Negro leader," addressing a gathering of Blacks in the hopes of quelling a riot, shouted consistently: "Mr. Charlie is armed baby! Them crackers is armed." A three-year-old black child in the best furnished home in the suburbs could interpret the connotations of such perjorative synonyms as "Mr. Charlie" and "crackers." These synonyms are a part of the language of Blacks from every avenue of American life. In order to communicate with each other in the presence of the master, the slaves developed a system of signs and images. The system survived the institution of slavery. And until James Baldwin's play, "Blues for Mr. Charlie," the language was incomprehensible to most white Americans. Due to Baldwin and to the courage of today's young black people who insist upon calling a cracker a cracker and a honkie a honkie out loud, white people have been made conscious of that metaphoric world of language in which they are condemned, castigated, and insulted by their porters, maids, countermen and orderlies. Now the world knows who Mr. Charlie is, and thus one of the most colorful symbols in the language has been negated.

The damage to the psyche is immeasurable. On the one hand, satisfaction is gained from mocking the enemy to his face while he, smiling all the while, sees in you only the stereotype of his American history. With a sense of joy, you vilify his family, race, and nation. On the other hand, you know that you must speak a language which he cannot comprehend; that you must wear "the minstrel's mask;" that you must guard against a slip of the tongue. Failure to do any of the above might bring down the apparatus, so carefully constructed by your ancestors during those first years on American soil, and bring about your own destruction in one way or another.

Fear provided the structure of the apparatus—the metaphorical language, the wide, timid smile, the Uncle Tom mannerisms—fear keeps the mechanism secret and intact; fear forces a minstrel's mask upon every Negro. He lives in the American society by repressing his true instincts, suppressing his anxieties, and rigidly holding his emotions in check. I believe that unconsciously many Blacks have harbored the desire to pick up a gun, walk out into the crowd, and shoot "as often and as long as one can." Instead, the Negro goes passively to his job, to the theatre, to the corner store.

Such desires, therefore, find satisfaction in the unconscious, and this satisfaction is registered most often in dream phenomena. In the unconscious there is little need for a special apparatus, symbols and metaphors designed to confuse whites; there is little need for fear. The Negro who dreams of murdering a white man is fulfilling a desire which he would not dare speculate upon in his waking moments. Conversely, the Black who dreams of being lynched by a mob, gives form and body to thoughts which have always been with him but which he has not dared to voice.

The meanings are ominous but clear. The only free Negro in America is a sleeping Negro. For in sleep, sublimated emotions are brought to the surface with a freedom impossible during waking hours. I have had such moments of freedom and I relate two of them here; not for the psychologically sophisticated, nor for the academic scholar, but because these two moments are perhaps the only ones in my life in which honestly, fearlessly, and with passion I could sincerely say with Goethe, "Verweile doch, du bist so schön."

This dream occurred in 1964 after a trip home to visit my family. My young sister was in a church play and I accompanied her to one of the performances. Because it was given during the Easter season, the play centered about the death of the Christ; and among the various stage props was a large oil portrait of Christ which stood in the center of the stage throughout the performance and around which the drama unfolded. During the rehearsal I sat fascinated by the portrait and, despite my atheistic views, was moved by the play. This was the first time I had been inside a church in fifteen years. Back in New York five days later, I had the following dream:

I found myself alone in the church, standing in the center aisle. The room was dimly lit by two lamps, one at the foot of the pulpit, the other, which gave forth a softer, yellower light was near the entrance. Shadows, grey, and ominous, descended upon the church, lighting momentarily—or so it seemed—the portrait of Christ, spraying it in garish colors: first white, then orange, then yellow. Moving slowly down the aisle to the foot of the pulpit, I stopped some few feet from the portrait.

They tell me, I thought, that I am made in your image. Yet I look at you, and I see the men who abuse me, who persecute me. I see the men who kill my children even before they are born: those children who you said were to come unto you. They say that you are my Saviour and you died for me. But if this is so, why did you not prove it, for certainly you must have known what would happen to me, what they would do to me. Why did you not once, just once, do something, anything, to prove that you acknowledged my existence? Why couldn't you have made one of your followers, one of those twelve—even he who was to betray you—why couldn't you have made one of them black? And if not that, then when you asked the people that day on the mountain to step forward, to come to you and be blessed, why couldn't one of those men have looked like me? And on that last day, when they nailed you up and left you with two men and you said to them, "This day you will be with me in Paradise," why couldn't one of those who were the lowest of men—why couldn't one of those have been like me? Trembling, I moved closer to the rostrum.

No, I thought, it's a lie, all of it! All these years we've been kept in slavery. Yes, for you are the greatest slave master of them all. You taught us to be good to our enemies, to love them, to forgive them. Holding out promises of a heaven, you tied our hands and made us weak. Your words and promises kept us in bondage, and prevented us from doing the things that those, truly made in your image, have done to us. And so, whenever we look at you, we see them. Whenever we bow down to you, praise you, we are really bowing to and praising those like you, those with blue eyes, blond hair, and white skin. Whenever we worship you, we are, in reality, worshipping them.

My hands trembled violently. Tears sprang to my eyes. I slammed my fist into the palm of my hand. Giant hands tore a scream from my throat.

Yes, you are their saviour. It is they to whom you came and for whom you shed your blood. To them you have given your rod, your staff, and your power to enslave me, to bend me to their will; your power to rob me of life. They are your chosen ones, I your outcast. Yes, and so let it be. Let me not be tied to you. Let me not believe in you. Only in this way can I be free. Only in this way can I possess that freedom which you have granted to them.

With you, there is no freedom for me! No, no freedom and no hope. There is no heaven and no salvation! And until that day when I break away from you, when I hate your blue eyes, blond hair, and white face—until that day, I cannot really and truly hate them. It must begin with you. So let it be now, at this minute, when I can look at you and see them and hate you both, and I do, I hate you, yes!

My legs gave way and I fell at the foot of the platform. Harsh, guttural sounds wracked my body. Several times, a sharp scream came from my lips to reverberate from the walls of the church. I awakened to the sound of my own screaming.

The second dream occurred a few weeks after the death of Malcolm X in 1965. Malcolm had represented something important to me. To say merely that he was a man is not to explain his enormous influence upon those who, like myself, have lost faith in an American dream of egalitarian democracy. He was the first acknowledged prophet of our era to preach the moral decadence of Western civilization, to bring to the conscience of black people the truth concerning that culture in which we seem bent on immersing ourselves, and to force us to question the idols which we had accepted without question from those who were said to be wiser than we, our leaders.

Despite our political persuasions, few of us had thought deeply about the country in which we found ourselves, about its people, history, and future. We accepted George Washington, Thomas Jefferson, and the other legendary founders of the "democracy" without considering the fact that their hands were wet with the blood of slaves. We accepted the words of the Constitution, notwithstanding the fact that this document, when first drawn up, excluded us from consideration; and that even later amendments which did include us, were purchased with the barrels of many rifles.

We believed in democracy without ever being its beneficiaries, in the dogma of Christianity without being accorded the elementary rights of a Christian, and in the conscience and good will of the American people, when the true nature of this conscience was revealed in lynchings, bombings, starvation, and acts of unbelievable torture. We believed the lies of the white writers, historians and missionaries who said that we had been rescued from a jungle, a nightmare of darkness called Africa from whence came the endless, monotonous, unproductive civilization of the tom-toms, where infested swamps and bushes hid fierce reptiles and savage beasts; and that this Africa was the other side of hell in contradistinction to this semi-paradise, this "Eden" to which we were transported.

Our desire was to be Americans, not understanding what that word connotes in the vocabulary of our short, yet gruelling history. So many millions dead, so many millions still dying, and yet like men possessed, we rushed towards assimilation, towards integration, negating history, denying the present, and completely oblivious to the future.

But this rush to be Americans was on a larger scale to become part of Western civilization which, we had been taught, was a product of Jewish and Christian thought derived from the intellectual and moral atmosphere of Athens where Socrates, Plato, and Aristotle held sway. We believed that scholar who wrote that "western civilization is but a footnote to Plato" and stood awed at the might of western thought, accomplishment, and success.

Like James Baldwin, we too admired symbols of Western achievement such as the cathedral at Chartres and hated our ancestors because they had not constructed it. Moreover, we traduced those ancestors who we were told were beating out weird mystical incantations upon hide-covered drums while the Hebrews were writing the great scriptures and the Greeks were producing timeless drama and thought. Not knowing who we were and afraid to attempt the discovery, we emulated those who were linked to the grandeur of the past by the color of their skins.

Some, like my father, never feared to explore that culture from which long-yesterday he had sprung. Yet even when the knowledge of the myth which had been foisted upon him was revealed he, like others, could not forsake the dream of somehow being close to those who knew the wisdom of Socrates, the prophetic utterances of Solomon, or the sociology of Karl Marx.

Much before Ralph Ellison, he wanted to be an American Negro, some hybrid form of animal, a cross between something made and manufactured in America and something which, because it is American, is linked, no matter how tenuously, to the antiquity of Greece and Rome.

A man of great perception, my father was still unable to arrive at the most objective of all truths: that the inheritors of Western civilization have betrayed their heritage. The ideals of democracy, freedom, and equality handed down from the most famous sons of Greece have been turned into a mockery by those who have shamelessly colonized and exploited half the world. The teachings of the prophets which form the bulwark of Western ethics and morality, have been used as a pretext to enslave some, to burn others in gas ovens, and to lynch still more.

The predecessors of those to whom the tenets of justice, mercy, and honor were bequeathed, have honored their ancestors by anointing history with the blood of millions whose only crime was meekness, passivity, and trust. Like the men of old who subjected their God to ridicule and spectacle before riddling his body with nails, these, their historical siblings, have never allowed the God to be peacefully interred; but have dug up his body time and again to be ridiculed once more, to be drenched in blood and sweat yet another time, and to have nails driven into his flesh by even stronger arms than before.

Malcolm unveiled this history before us. "The white man is a devil!" he thundered. And in that statement is the most sincere indictment of Western civilization since that mob, in the shadow of the cross, broke into spontaneous applause as the martyr dropped his head upon his chest for the last time.

Moreover, Malcolm forced us to look at that with which we would integrate, to examine the history of those with whom we would assimilate, and to carefully observe this "burning house," which we sought so ardently, vigorously, and persistently to enter. He raised profound questions of morality, which our white anointed leaders refused to raise, and propounded the truth that not even the alleged savagery of our ancestors, those cannibals who ate other men, could stand equal to the acts performed by those who are purportedly the blessed of the Gods.

Malcolm thus sowed within our fertile minds the seeds of discontent—not with our treatment in the American society, such seeds had long ago blossomed into fruit—but with the idea of being part of all that has been instrumental in the wanton destruction of life, degradation of dignity, and contempt for the spirit. He caused us to question not what democracy could be but what it was; not the potential of Christianity but the actuality; not the ideals of western culture but the reality; not the thoughts of the prophets but the practice of these thoughts. In so doing, Malcolm became more than just a representative of "black masculinity"; he became the embodiment of an idea: that the new Canaan will not be built by those who are called the children of God but rather by those to whom the God in his apocalyptic fury never came.

I stood before a microphone. I was dressed in an African agbada, blue in color and embroidered in gold. A man stood on each side of me. Both were dressed in white robes with black cummerbunds. Beyond the speakers' platform were, it seemed, thousands of people, black and white, some standing, some sitting, and some supported by some invisible force. Before this assembled multitude, I stood secure and comfortable. Somewhere in the back of the hall a voice shouted: "Indictment!" For the first time, I looked down at the notebook opened on the stand before me, flipped a page and began to speak.

"Two weeks ago, four black children were murdered by bombs in this country. Like a fountain, the American conscience turned on, gushing out sympathy and anger. Yes, for approximately two weeks, the fountain bubbled forth. And then, suddenly, the faucet shut down and the incident was forgotten.

"Now we can assume—no, we can predict—that this is what white people will do time and again, for this is what white people have always done. They have short memories! But can we assume that Blacks too will forget? Can any Jew forget Auschwitz and Dachau? No, they cannot and we cannot. Yet our Negro leaders say that we will forget; no, not only forget but also forgive. Now these are those Negro leaders that are called responsible, and I for one, must ask to whom they are responsible?

"They are not responsible to black people for all they ask of us is our patience, our tolerance, aud our lives. And all this they ask in the name of God, truth, and right. We know too well how their argument runs: we are morally superior to those who butcher us, capable of loving them and thereby inoculating them with love so that one day love too will grow in their hearts and minds. This, supposedly, will happen because God is on our side. But what black man sitting here today can claim that God is on our side? How many of us believe that he stands beside us? Well, maybe so, but if so, then he stands not beside us but behind us; yes like a snivelling coward, behind us.

"Yes, because the white bigots have gotten to him too! They have frightened their God, and so we will get no help from him. But perhaps we can rely on the truth. But the truth is what white people say it is. And this is so because they have the power to make it so. And what is this power? It is nothing more than the power of life and death. There is no greater power that one man can have over another. So, my quarrel with the Negro leaders is that they have delegated that power exclusively to whites.

"Their dedication to love, God, and morality has given those who today destroy us, a covering of immunity. For we have been neutralized, our hands bound, while others commit murders and atrocities upon us. The Negro leaders have helped to make black life the most inexpensive commodity in this country." I paused for the first time. Unconscious of time, it was as though I had said all of this and much more in the space of a few seconds. I wiped my face and flipped another page in my notebook.

"But my friends, white people have been deluded! They are still deluded. We black people must not allow ourselves to be deluded also. Let us not be deluded about the American conscience. I spoke of this conscience as being like a faucet and we know that when a faucet is shut off you don't know whether there is any water there or not. It may be dry. And so when the Negro leaders say that we will tap the American conscience, maybe there is nothing there to be tapped. Perhaps the truth is that the American people have run dry of decency, justice, and tolerance. And so from their hearts and minds, as barren as the driest deserts, we will get nothing; and until we realize that there is nothing there to get, we will remain deluded." I paused to flip another page.

"But white people too are deluded; and their delusion is by far the greater. You know they always call us boys and girls. No matter what our age, they regard us as children. And why is this? The reason is because we are children. Only children, boys and girls, allow themselves to be slapped down again and again by the enraged parent; only children bend their knees and dream of a thunderbolt from the sky; only children give up the power of life; the power not only to die for something but also to kill for it! Yes, to kill for it!

"Yes! For this is what it means to be a man in a world where there is no justice, where the law is prostituted, yes, to be a man and not a child is to hold the power of life and death. And we will remain children until we take this power and use it. Yes, I say use it! Let the necks of white people crack under the pressure of the hangman's rope; let their flesh feel the sting, the force of hot, burning balls of metal; let their blond-haired, blue-eyed boys feel the knife cutting into their insides, slicing away the instruments of manhood.

"Ah, some of my white friends are twitching in their seats! How shocked, how sickened, how very frightened you are. But you have listened to the Negro leaders and so it has never occurred to you that I have always wanted to do to you what you have done to me. But haven't you given me that right, shown me that only through violence can we communicate, man to man?

"Yes, in a thousand ways you have. It is your blueprint which stands before me. Yours is the example of what it means to be a man! Has it never occurred to you, never entered your mind, that that one dream of my life, salvation, will come for me when I cease to be a child and become a man on your terms: a man willing not only to die for freedom, but to kill for it? No, this has never occurred to you and therefore this, this, is your delusion." I stepped away from the rostrum. The two men who had remained at my side throughout, stepped forward to shake my hand. "My brothers," I said, and woke up to the ringing of the alarm clock.

13

BLACK FATHERS AND

THEIR SONS

Part I

"I am sorry," wrote a friend, "for using a letter to you as an excuse for shedding so much sickness." Our weekly letters had been therapeutic nostrums for both of us. In these letters we breached that barrier between truth and half truth which always stood between us in any meaningful dialogue with the white world. We had flaunted our sickness, owned up to it, offered no apologies for our despair, our feelings of hopelessness, of hatred, of bitterness. For the first time, perhaps, we had acted as men: that is, vomited forth our truth, as every man must inevitably do.

For a long time, however, this was difficult. We had not trusted each other at first. Meeting in a graduate classroom of a large white university, we were both suspicious as to how the other had gotten there. How many timid-Negro grins had we bestowed on white professors in our respective undergraduate schools? How many of those white professors had we succeeded, using our black skins as artillery, in frightening out of a grade? How many other Blacks had we left pulsating on the floor, as we hurriedly trampled over them for academic favors?

But more important: How many roles had we been forced to play? On what day, Uncle Tom, on what day, the Militant New Negro, and which of these roles had stuck with us, subconsciously clung to us, undiscernible to whites, yet glaringly revealed to any

Negro? These things we had to find out about each other before either of us could be free to indulge his sickness.

For Negroes, to even engage in speculations about whites demands serious scrutinization of one's audience. If one's view is liberal, one is open to the charge of Uncle Tomism. If one's view is hostile, one is censured as militant. Each censure carries the same punishment: ostracism. Thus Negroes in first meetings with one another must invariably wade through hours of meaningless dialogue, pretend the role of devil's advocate, quote profusely from both sides of the race question until one finally arrives at a decision as to the stand of one's companion.

My friend and I were diametrically opposed; and yet, despite this, we were united in our mutual unhealthy frame of mind. He had been brought up in the Booker T. Washington tradition: taught to believe that one could solve the problem of color by building a bigger ranch house than his neighbor. His parents had demanded of him that he excel, that he always come in first in the race, and those occasions on which he ran a poor second, he was severely chastised. His early life was one of continuous libraries, concerts, and weekly sermons at an educated Baptist minister's church. At thirteen years of age he read Dickens, Tolstoy, and Emerson. At sixteen he wrote his first essay: "A tribute to Abraham Lincoln."

At seventeen years of age he graduated from high school, first in a class of one hundred and fifty, and four years later, he graduated from college, *summa cum laude*. Now, for the first time in his life, he was away from home, away from the watchful and protective eyes of middle class Negro parents, in a situation where firsts were as common as grains of sand.

My life had been entirely different. Exactly what my philosophical orientation was is difficult to tell. I was torn between two conflicting ideologies, and like Faust, I was inseparably bound to both proponents of these ideologies. My mother was immersed in the dogma of Christianity, and my father was submerged in the dogma of Karl Marx.

Somewhere in the early stages of my existence they had decided that each was to have a crack at me. I was subjected to Jesus Christ at nine o'clock on Sunday mornings, after which I was free to leave church and go to the vacant lot, next to a poolroom, where my father ministered every Sunday to the irreligious masses. It was as though I were Adam in the Garden of Eden and Gabriel and Satan were wrestling for my soul. At the outset, my mother had the inside track. Having been bribed (a dollar if I read it from cover to cover) into reading the Bible, I shared much of my mother's enthusiasm for Christianity. The stories of the creation and the revelation held a fascination for me, although I suppose that even then I was being unloyal to my mother's teaching: I had more than an underdog's sympathy for Satan; and I was more convinced that Judas was a victim of historical determinism than a conscious villain.

Nevertheless, my fondness for my mother coupled with her bribes early won me to her side. My father did nothing outwardly to counteract her influence. Shrewder than my mother and more pragmatic, he knew that the philosophy of Christianity when confronted by the realities of my own experiences would be proven untenable on its own merits. "No thinking Negro," he once remarked, "can remain a Christian." More principled than my mother, he offered no bribes. He bought me books written by Negroes and instead of coaxing me to read them, he put faith in his evaluation of my own inquisitive nature to propel me in that direction in a way which a monetary bribe could not.

As a result, by the age of thirteen I had read *Souls of Black Folk* by W.E.B. DuBois, the autobiographies of Frederick Douglass and Booker T. Washington, poems by Langston Hughes, the Carter G. Woodson series on Negro Life and History, and novels by Richard Wright, Claude McKay, and Jesse Fauset. In addition, from his well stocked collection of Russian literature, I read, on my own, the Russian Masters: Pushkin, Gogol, Tolstoy, Chekhov, Turgenev, Dostoyevsky.

None of my reading of this material was accompanied by lectures from my father. Whereas my mother had thought it necessary to illustrate the truth of the Bible through symbolism and metaphor, my father, on the other hand, was content to let me arrive at my own truth. He had no doubt, in his own mind, as to what that truth would be. Convinced of the wrongness of the cause of Christianity and knowing that, as a way of life, Christianity could not survive the test of time, he felt that automatically, through despair, I would gravitate towards communism as he had.

The road to communism lay in a process of elimination, wherein one discarded capitalism in favor of this higher truth. It was as though he conceived of the world of the Negro as being enclosed only by these two philosophies. Capitalism, he stressed, was irrelevant to the Negro. In a world composed of bourgeois elements and proletarian elements all, despite the claims of the petit-bourgeoisie among them, were members of the proletariat. "Communism," he once wrote, "means, in a simplistic sense, the dictatorship of the proletariat. We Negroes are the proletariat; all we need is the dictatorship."

Thus the route to truth, led through the negation of the philosophy of Christianity (to him capitalism and Christianity were one and the same), a cleansing, as he used the biblical phrase, of one's "sinful soul." Like Keats, he saw truth as beauty and, to paraphrase Samuel Coleridge, Communism as the divine ventriloquist through which that truth was made manifest: it became word, then flesh, then spirit. Despite his pragmatism, in this sense he was as romantic as my mother; although his romanticism had been manufactured out of a sense of despair.

A Negro intellectual in the thirties, his only choice was escapism or despair. Negroes were lynched at the rate of one every week; black children in the schools, both segregated as in the South and integrated as in some parts of the North, were then, as now, cast like refuse upon the junkheap of American Society. Race riots in which men, women, and children were brutally, murdered and maimed were common occurrences in the North and South. Furthermore, the depression had hit hardest at the Negro, especially those in urban areas. Black men, often with children at their sides, stood in lines awaiting the dispensing of foodstuffs—sacks of meal, small white navy beans, and slabs of fat back (white, salted meat)—forced to bow and scrape before the white overseers of the program, or more frequently, to relinquish their position in line to late arriving whites.

Despite personal knowledge to the contrary, the Negro intellectual was forced to ask, in his private soul, with W.E.B. DuBois, suppose all that they say about us is really true? Suppose the descendants of Thomas Nelson Page and Thomas Dixon, who argue that the black man's inferior position in the world is due to biological laws, the laws of nature immutable and unchangeable unless through the process of complete assimilation—suppose, after all, this is true.

Surely the objective evidence pointed to the Afro-American's inferiority. The lowest I.Q. scores were made by Blacks. The slowest students in the school system were black. Black people had not built the great cathedrals, designed the mammoth bridges, discovered the great cures for disease, written the immortal literature. No Afro-American sat in the high councils of government, nor occupied any real seat of power. Furthermore, no Black then, as now, was out of the reach of white power: neither the uncontrolled fury of the lynch mob, nor the controlled fury of a racist policeman.

Confronted with this wall of insurmountable facts, the Negro intellectual was forced to look within, forced to take the excursion into self where truth reigned undistorted. Whatever calm, whatever peace was to be found by rejecting the outer reality and clinging to an inner subjective reality which could not be proven, either to the bigoted skeptics or more important, to one's loved ones: wife and child. Proudly, Ulysses remarks in Tennyson's poem by that name: "I have become a man!" Such a statement could not have been passed on from a black father to his son. For the black Telemachuses were wise children. They knew where the seat of power lay, knew their oppressors, and knew and resented the helplessness of their fathers.

The father was impotent, if not cowardly, in their eyes; somehow the father was blamed for the present, held responsible for the past, and dismissed as an important element in whatever the future would bring. At that level it was impossible to understand him, and easy to hate him. It was not important to the child that the father had not built the great cathedrals or created the great literature. What was important, however, was that the father had not torn down the signs which read "white" or "black" on the walls of public rest rooms, on public drinking fountains, and on buses and street cars. Moreover, the father had given them legal-ity, had, in effect, acquiesced in his own emasculation, by peaceful, passive compliance.

My father, I believe, felt this dual contempt—one from the outside world, the other from his son—more than most. At times he would look at me with disdain, perhaps reading something in my eyes that I could not imagine to be there. Though we were the best of friends, and I loved and respected him deeply, he knew that in reality we were enemies. I was the young Hamlet who sooner or later would be forced to thrust the dagger into his heart, forced to stamp out his life in order to be free of the guilt which I felt, and would feel, so long as he lived. For me he would have had to die to become a man; take a hammer, go forth and rip down those infamous signs, be shot in the process, in order to give life to me.

He knew what I felt for he too had deserted the God of his father. "My father," he once remarked, "was a weak, spineless man asking the white God to do the things that he didn't have the courage to do himself." He knew that these were the words which I would eventually hurl at him. Out of his despair, like his father, he had taken unto himself a God, asked it to perform miracles, to open the gate to the promised land, to smite his enemies, to release his children from bondage, to let his people go.

After having seen the world go down in death, doom, and destruction he had accepted a new God, in an attempt to assure himself that life would go on, that order would once again be restored, that optimism was not yet dead. And in this respect he was like my mother. Neither could believe in futility, neither could postulate an existence devoid of the props, the machinery of infantile optimism; each in his own way placed more faith than he should have in the human species, in man, in his ability to transcend, to treat his fellow man as another human being with Christ, or as an integral part of any possible society with Marx.

Both veered towards this common faith and belief in mankind; and both, at this point, believed in conversion. The sinner could be saved, the oppressor redeemed, the executioner transformed. Mankind had, despite historical evidence to the contrary, the inner strength and conviction to build the great society in which all men would live free and unmolested by outer forces. Neither believed in a complete philosophy of nihilism, neither would have supported the argument of Turgenev's Bazarov that I don't know what comes after, and I don't care, I only know that what exists now must be destroyed. Neither would go that far, neither would throw optimism to the winds in exchange for complete negativism; neither would believe the fallen angel to have fallen below the level of redemption. For both this was an area beyond their comprehension, and for this reason perhaps, both would awaken to the sad truth that in the quest for my soul both would be losers.

True to her Christian upbringing, my mother took the fact of my betrayal with stoic suffering. Sometimes now, I suppose, she still prays for me, hoping that the prodigal will—if not return to the house of his God—at least find peace. My father on the other hand took defeat very hard. Partly it was due to the guilt which he harbored for having forsaken his own father; partly it was because he was shrewd enough to know that every Black Hamlet, like himself, had held a knife poised at the breast of a father, and that only by acquiescing in the death of the father could the son be free. But more important, in rejecting his philosophy, I was, in a sense, rejecting his attempt to convince me of his manhood, telling him in effect that he was not at war with society, but instead engaged in a mock skirmish in which no decisive victories could be won. I was throwing all his theories into disrepute, telling him that the process of negation was an unsure one, that a communist heaven was as bad as a Christian one, and that perhaps, the alternatives to both heavens was hell.

At sixteen years of age, I unsheathed the dagger. Having been selected as a finalist in an oratorical contest, I chose as my subject: "The Myth of Gods." In the speech I attacked Christianity, democracy, and Communism, saving my heaviest criticism for Communism. "Just," I said in words which would rankle within my father's conscience, "as Christianity was spawned by white men, so will Communism or any ism be spawned by white men; to believe, then, that one will work, when the other will not, though both have the same mother is to be unrealistic; no gods spawned from the brains of white men can do other than enslave black men; we must therefore rid ourselves of all the white gods, regardless of what names they go by." I had opened the wound. In the audience, my father looked up at me, frowned, and shook his head. That night, alone in the living room, the wound was opened further. "You can't go through life hating every one," he said, "believing in nothing; your speech was a speech of hatred. You denigrate the human race, all of it; this should not be. You must never lose sight of what is good in men, of what is beautiful in the human spirit. Life is a challenge, not a formula already set down for someone to build a paradise upon; no, one must work for paradise; one must work for a good world; and one must believe in people, for people will make this world."

"You sound like Momma;" I retorted: "And this is your problem; your God is no blacker than hers, your paradise no nearer than hers, your prophets no more accurate than hers. Perhaps both of you need Gods; perhaps all the black people in this country, need Gods; but I don't. I don't need any Gods; for having forsaken Momma's God, I have forsaken all Gods."

We would continue to be friends, although the bond of father-son had been irreparably severed. His world was as dead to me as was the world of my mother. I was orphaned, with nothing to comfort me, to warm me, but the dagger of my mind. I was alone, a voluntary outcast, alienated from those whom I deeply loved, at an age when no young man should be alone. Unlike Faust, I had refused to sell my soul, perhaps, because I believed neither in God nor the devil. Furthermore, I believed, as my father had said, in nothing. Like Bigger Thomas, my life, to quote Baldwin, "was surrounded by hate." However, more sophisticated than Bigger Thomas, I did not release my frustrated hatred by killing—perhaps I would have undergone a healthy catharsis by doing so. But I did not. I moved in a world of shadows, incomprehensible to anyone but me. I sought for values within, conscious of the fact that I would have to make my own; that there was no blueprint for me to follow.

I knew what every Hamlet knows; that the values by which the father lives are untransferable; and if the Hamlet is black this is even truer. Each black child must dig his own way out of the mud and stench of twentieth century life, must create his own values; and no black father can hand his values down to his son. I believe that my father, too, recognized this, despite the fact that he could never bring himself to admit it. Like all revolutionaries, he was committed to revolution only on his terms. To argue that the social order needed to be destroyed was to him indicative of one's intelligence and progressivism; on the other hand, to suggest that his blueprint for the reconstruction of society was not the right one, was to indicate reaction and ignorance.

Moreover, to suggest, as I had done, that the father was not, and could not be the guiding light, the shining beacon heralding the advent of the son into the world, was treacherous. And for this he never forgave me. It was not that he became rude, or antagonistic towards me; he simply became indifferent. He read my essays on Negro novelists, scrutinized my short stories, and listened to my recitals of speeches on the American Democracy for high school classes. Yet all of this he did as a critic, completely objective, holding his opinions within. By the time I graduated from high school, we had become almost totally estranged. Communication had broken down; it was as if we were separated by a gulf which transcended the years, a gulf spanning the very history of the Negro's relationship to society and his fellow man. We had found out things about each other, things of the spirit, which had made us incompatible as father and son.

Despite his radicalism, for him the spirit of the times and of his soul was the spirit of western humanism emanating from the Greek city state to the present day. Urbane and sophisticated, he would have fitted into the turbulent times of the eighteenth century, not as a black man but as a white man. For him, therefore, it was not a search for identity but simply being able to hold onto his identity against those who would rob him of it. A leader, he was as far from his followers in temperament, hopes, fears, and anxieties as the pretender to the British throne from his fellow countrymen, and it was to his credit that he refrained from evidencing disgust or contempt for followers who would not make good citizens, even in his own utopia.

My argument against him was that he had misjudged both the spirit of the times and the spirit of his own soul. How he could adhere to the philosophy of the enlightenment was beyond me; and how he could have sacrificed his integrity in clinging to an identity vouchsafed by a society which was but the result of a tradition which he should have hated and despised I could not understand.

Long before James Baldwin and Lorraine Hansberry, I had decided that I did not want to be integrated into a burning house. More specifically, I wanted to be instrumental in setting that house aflame, in watching it burn to a crisp. My spirit was more than revolutionary, for each revolutionary is necessitated by the dogma which produces him to present an alternate plan, to build a better mousetrap than the one which he would displace.

No such strictures bound me. Having decided through empirical evidence—the day by day experience of being black in America—that my condition was the worst, my interests were simply in ameliorating that condition; if my condition were indeed the worst, then no plan was necessary, what came after was academic. The country should be set to flames, gutted from one city to another, and the survivors should sit atop the dying embers and dream of the new society. But the dream was possible only after —not before—the apocalypse had occurred.

These are the views which earlier separated me from my father, and later separated me from my friend in graduate school. Like my father, he too was more "Anglo Saxon than the Anglo Saxons." His world was the world of Jefferson, Emerson, Hemingway, and Faulkner by way of default. He studied these men, and in studying them formed a mystical union between himself and them which gave him a badge in the society. He never questioned the fact that he was wed to corpses, that the thoughts and ideas of his heroes were thoughts not applicable to millions of black men, and therefore not applicable to him. He had never been able to think in such terms.

Like my father, he thought, in terms of a cosmology which included all mankind, irrespective of the fact that other Blacks were not included in this select club. The exclusion of his brothers did not bother him, however. What bothered him most of all was the fact that they (other Negroes) remained as a constant embarrassment to him. The rioting by black people throughout the country cast him in a new light, made him visible to his white friends who had previously found his disquisitions on Wordsworth, Pope, and Shelley to be illuminating. Now they wanted his opinions on Negroes, on the riots, on the possibility of wide-scale violence between black and white.

Against his will he was called upon to interpret the black revolution, and none of his friends realized that he was incapable of doing so. The gulf between himself and the black rioters was a very wide one, widened over the years by his family and friends, each attempting to convince him that the concept of Negritude was a joke, that man was an individual, and that no man's fate was inexplicably bound to that of another. He had, because of this, become a man with no allegiance, a man with no real identity, estranged in a society where the words individuality and brotherhood constantly clash with one another.

Yet, in being called upon to interpret a new phenomenon, one of which he knew very little, he was destined, in the course of his explorations, to confront the realities of his existence as a black man in the American society. For the first time he was forced to examine the concept "Negro Intellectual" and see behind the concept the vicious categorization in microcosm of what was more full blown in the life of the average Afro-American. For a "Negro Intellectual," like a "Negro Leader," was a special brand of Negro, yet, Negro nonetheless. The teachers who had singled him out as a "brilliant young Negro" were paying him a left handed compliment, creating for him a special class in order to be able to more accurately distinguish him from the all inclusive class into which his black skin had placed him. Yet over and above him stood that class for which all of his training had prepared him, towards which his mother and father in their constant cajolings had pushed him, to which on the strength of intellect, accomplishment, and ability he duly belonged.

He therefore realized, for the first time, how complete his rejection really was, and too, he realized the extent of his alienation. He was, to paraphrase Mathew Arnold, a wanderer between two worlds, one he wanted dead and the other he was powerless to bring to life. Somehow fate had cheated him. He was equipped to be white in everything but skin color, and to the deepest part of him, he desired to be white. He was convinced that western civilization was God's greatest gift to man, and that only those capable of being a part of western civilization were deserving of the appelation civilized. Unlike James Baldwin he would have had no perplexing problems in looking upon the Chartres Cathedral. He would have taken it for his own, mainly because of his ability to interpret its beauty, gazed upon it with the scrutiny of a scholar and felt a common bond between himself and its creator.

Yet he would awaken to the horrible reality that the Chartres Cathedral was not for the likes of him. No knowledge of the great works of antiquity—of Aeschylus, Homer, Sophocles, Milton, Chaucer—could compensate for his black skin. The society had created one measuring rod by which to gauge him, one criteria by which to determine his worth, one set of guidelines to define his humanity, and in so doing relegated him forever and despite all to a special niche in its own cosmological scheme.

And none of his "firsts" could help him! How many times must he have sat—as all Blacks sometimes sit—alone in seclusion with his private soul and reflected on the contradictions inherent in this society. He had been told that diligence, application, and perseverence were the pathways to dignity and recognition as a human being. Manhood, he had thought, was to be earned by testing oneself against those supposedly one's equal, beating them in those pursuits supposedly their private domain. This he had done and his brilliant record supported the assertion. He was not only good enough to be among them, but in most cases good enough to be above them.

Yet day by day he was threatened by those same monsters which beset every black man in America: his dignity was affronted by the corner clerk, called into question by a taxicab driver, denied by a white laborer on any public transportation, and annihilated by any racist policeman. He was as helpless, as trapped, as victimized as any Negro, in any ghetto, in any part of the country; yet, he was limited in a way in which they were not. He was not free to burn down buildings, to man the rooftops and snipe at his oppressors, to wield the broken bottle, to hurl the cold, crumbling brick. Still holding to the dream, he was unable, like Bigger Thomas, to even blunder into manhood by taking another life, by being destructive, by releasing the pent up emotion now beginning to come to the surface of his conscience.

The society which had conditioned him to believe that he was different, that he was not like other Negroes, that he was a special case, had helped to transform him into a sick, frustrated, neurotic young man: a Dr. Jekyll-Mr. Hyde personality in which the two opposing identities could not always be precariously balanced. As Dr. Jekyll, he yearned for recognition from white America, courted its approval, desired its benevolence; as Mr. Hyde he desired destruction, courted violence, and wished for, perhaps, self annihilation. The key to his survival, then, would lie in his ability to maneuver between these two roles, to shift identity at will, yet to be always conscious that he was shifting roles, to insure that he would not inadvertently become Dr. Jekyll forever—an identity which could only lead to further confrontations with reality—nor become Mr. Hyde for all times—a role which would lead him to either cut his throat or dedicate himself to nihilism.

Like my father, perhaps he was destined to become a piteous old man existing on a dream because to let go of the dream was to court disaster. He too saw salvation in terms of a white God, irrespective of the facts of history that all white Gods had succeeded in betraying their black subjects. Neither he nor my father would allow himself the luxury of complete, everlasting hatred, the surrender of the soul forever, for eternity to that Mr. Hyde part which dared to thunder forth the incontestable statement: This is the worst.

Idealists destined for senseless martyrdom, theirs would always be the world of inaction, of stagnation, of frustration. They shouted for freedom when what they really wanted was respect; they clamored for equality when what they really sought was recognition. If the scholars bred in the tradition of Western civilization were to write their epitaphs they would accord them special niches among the martyred. For me, however, they have written their own epitaphs. They were children in a world which cries out for men; they were dreamers in a world in which only the nightmare has reality, they were liars in a world which needs truth; they were conservatives at a time when revolutionaries are necessary; they were martyrs, and like all martyrs they deserved their crosses.

Yet, in his last letter, my friend had begun to realize the extent of his sickness, and this may yet save him from the cross. However, he had only reached purgatory: the realization. Heaven: the acting upon the realization, lay some many years in the future. Perhaps, like my father, he will never get to heaven; perhaps he will remain for the rest of his life in purgatory warring with shadows instead of concrete, material things—I do not really know. I stopped writing to him because I could not communicate with spirits in purgatory; we were too far apart, too great a gulf separated his purgatorial world from my heavenly one; yet that he could ever reach my heaven is doubtful. To do so he would have to be born again, undergo the transformation from adult to childhood and begin the long road upward. He would have to find his identity not in Western Civilization but in that mutilated species of humanity which Franz Fannon has called the wretched of the earth. In short, he would have to become black in mind, body, and soul.

Thirteen years ago, I sat in my father's small book-filled room looking up at this tired man who, I knew, still bore the scar of my dagger. We did not look each other squarely in the face, perhaps because he realized that there was no longer an equality between us. The roles had been changed. I was on my way to becoming the man that he had never been able to be, free in a way far beyond his wildest expectations. He was old, decrepit and dispirited, clinging to life with that same selfish tenacity with which he had clung to his dream: that tomorrow the world would be better, and thus a good place in which to die. "I hope," he said to me, hardly above a whisper, "that when you finish your education, you will go out and help your people, educate them, as I have tried to do."

"No," I replied, staring at him, searching for those eyes which he kept hidden from me; "No, I will not try to educate them; they will educate me. Perhaps they will teach me to make fire-bombs, and give me the strength and courage to throw them at the nearest slum building. I will go to them, not to teach, but to learn—to learn the things that no white God could ever teach me."

We said nothing more after that. Now and then he attempted to scan my face, to catch me unaware, and look into my eyes, but he could not bring himself to make the face to face confrontation. He would probably have liked to assure himself that I was not really his son, that I was some stranger, sent to betray his faltering eyesight. Even then he could not forego illusion in an attempt to deny reality. He saw not me, but a shadow, and that shadow was unreal, incomprehensible, and strange. I left shortly after kissing him on the cheek, and grasping his hand in a pretense at affection. I did not see him alive again; he died six weeks later, the world no better nor worse than the day he was born.

14

BLACK FATHERS AND

THEIR SONS

Part II

I DID NOT CRY at my father's funeral. Standing between my sister and aunt, trying not to look at the waxen figure before me, I folded and unfolded my arms, stared down at my feet and up at the faces of black people who had come to say good-by to him. The reason that I did not cry had nothing to do with our recent estrangement. We needed each other too much to have remained estranged for long. There was no question of my love for him, for I loved him very much even though he did things which pained me deeply.

I was not sorry that he was dead! That may not have been my expressed opinion at the time, for I was young and not yet so cynical. I realize now that not only was I not sorry that he was dead, but I looked upon his death as a blessing. I am no longer young; and I am now quite cynical. In this respect, I am different from my father. I cannot recall his ever uttering a cynical remark. In fact, he reserved his bitterest criticism for cynics. "They are men who believe that reality is fixed and cannot be changed;" he often said, "and when one reaches that conclusion about the world, he can never change anything; he is better off dead."

Perhaps. I believed that a great deal depended upon whether one considered reality to be worth changing. My father, on the other hand, assumed that a world in which men were victims of institutions and governments needed changing; and he would accept neither oppressors nor oppressed as fixed realities in a world ruled by men. Both oppressed and oppressor, he believed, were the products of corrupt governments and institutions; and he would not allow governments or institutions to define reality for him. A student of Jean Jacques Rousseau, he believed in the innate goodness of man. He saw the city state as the first community of man to be organized around a political leader. Corruption set in when, out of a desire to unite their community with God, the religious scribes attributed divine power to the political leader. The king was anointed, and at that moment man lost the privilege of defining reality for himself. For the duty of the king, to paraphrase Plato, is to define reality for his subjects.

In my father's peculiar cosmological system, however, the king was not responsible for encroaching upon the freedom of his subjects—the system that spawned the king was culpable. Power corrupts to be sure, but whether the corruption is absolute or relative depends upon the allegiance one owes to his fellow man. The power of the king was not vouchsafed by the people. It was his by divine right. Therefore, the king's allegiance was not to the people but to the divine order of things. The solution was not complex. Behead the king and destroy the divine order. Thus power would pass to the people and they, free to construct their own universe, would set about defining themselves.

My father had been drugged by the opiate of Marxism. He was a romantic in a world where mankind metes out its harshest punishment to romantics and martyrs. He was the forerunner of those who today shout "Power to the people," although he was far more honorable than they. He sincerely wished to see power placed in the hands of the masses; even though he realized that the moment the masses obtained power, intellectuals like himself would be among the first to be assigned to the wall.

Part of our difficulty with one another stemmed from his romanticism. He was so romantic about people and the world around him that for a long time I believed him to be mad. A forceful orator, he was often called upon to speak on behalf of the Communist Party; but, privately or publicly, his speeches always contained references to the coming revolution in which the American people, rising as one, would throw off oppression and unite under the banner of brotherhood. He did not believe in separatism, and although he often castigated "Mr. Charlie" with the vehemence of a Malcolm X, his was a dream in which black, yellow, brown and white men walked shoulder to shoulder in unity.

We are indebted to Franz Fanon for predicting the coming war between the haves and the have-nots, between the machine men and the natural men. My father reached a similar conclusion in the 1940's. In his speeches he argued that the have-nots would engage the haves in a bloody revolution and that the have-nots who outnumbered the haves, would finally win. Like some black militants at the present time, he believed in an alliance of black and white radicals, and his allegiance to the Communist Party was due, in part, to the fact that it made such an alliance possible.

This constituted the most irrational and romantic aspect of his philosophy. Even at the age of nineteen, I was suspicious of alignments with white people. When I questioned his judgment on this point, he was quick to answer that "many white people were more revolutionary than black people," which proved nothing to me except that, even in the area of revolution and rebellion, whites were accorded a greater degree of freedom than Blacks. He was so obsessed with the desire to remake the world, to march at the head of an integrated revolution, that, unlike Richard Wright, he failed to understand the full implication of the American-Soviet pact in 1942. In an act of expediency, the Communist Party decided to "lay the Negro question aside" at a time when one black man was lynched in America every day. Today the Communist Party is the greatest opponent of Black Nationalism.

"Those who ignore history are doomed to repeat it," wrote Bismarck. The statement was meant for those who survive history, not those who perish. The children of men who have survived the holocaust, who managed to come through unscathed, soon forget that they are descendants of victims, that oppression was leveled against their fathers, and pledge undying fealty to god and country.

The reason is clear. Each man recoils in horror at the idea that the term victim might be applied to him. No man wants to be a victim nor admit that he is one. To be Emperor of Rome is far more satisfying than to be impaled upon the bloody nails of the cross. The children of victims begin to fantasize about oppression: Tyranny was always directed against some other people, some other race, some other group of dissenters. The chances are that such people brought damnation upon their own heads. They pushed the government too far, contested the wrong decisions of the majority group, or, more likely, deserved the punishment they received.

I remember a Japanese professor, an expert on brain disease working with monkeys which he had come to prefer to people, standing in his laboratory at the University of California, the tears running down his face, asking "Why did they lock me up? They took me out of school and locked me up. Why me?"

He addressed the question to me. The Indians could have given him a better answer. These first victims of American oppression evidence how far Americans will travel along the road to racial genocide. The Indian population once outnumbered that of many nations in the world today. That population has been depleted like the herds of buffalo which once supplied the Indians with food. Today the children of the holocaust live on the largesse of the children of their persecutors, packed on reservations, hungry men in a land of affluence. To those who deign to listen, the folklore and dances of the Indian people tell of persecution unsurpassed in the annals of human history.

Theirs, however, is the history of the victim and men want no part of it. Like the Japanese professor, they are content to live secure in the belief that times have changed, that the new Americans are different from the old, that the tyrant has reformed; until one day the bubble bursts, reality transplants illusion, and one is forced to ask the question "Why me?" The answer given by the historian is not likely to be the true one. The victim lives history, seldom does he write it. Those to whom this task is entrusted are usually master distorters, more concerned with appearance than actuality. If one reads American history textbooks, for example, *The Epic of America* by James Truslow Adams, he is likely to wonder why the Indians were not slaughtered to the man. They were savages incapable of building the great society, uncultured, uncivilized, content to allow the wealth of America to remain underground. Stumbling blocks in the path of progress, they deserved their fate; and a nation ordained by God to establish life, liberty and the pursuit of happiness on earth, measured out their fate with the barrels of many rifles.

Are men ignorant of such facts of history as the genocide of the Indians? Not ignorant, naive! In the nineteen-forties when the symbol of man's reality was the concentration camp, when one black man was lynched every day, my father remained convinced that black people would not be exterminated *en masse* by white Americans. Naiveté knows no time barrier. Today, when the American government exploits South Americans, napalms Vietnamese, and keeps half the world in ignorance and poverty, some Blacks refuse to believe that they will fall victim to similar acts of persecution.

"Black people," I wrote at the age of nineteen, "are a people alone; we have no allies and no friends. We face the darkness alone." My father, upon reading these words, became very angry. He realized that I was challenging his concept that each man but for corrupt governments and institutions would be his brother's keeper. He answered me in the usual way; that is, he flaunted his knowledge and ridiculed my ignorance. "What do you know," he shouted, "what do you know about allies? I know about allies! I know that we have allies! Look at Russia, look at China, look at the workers in every country of the world." I did not reply. There are those illusions which men must retain in order to hold on to their sanity. Had there been no Marx, he would have become as devout a follower of Christ as he became of the author of *Das Kapital*. As it was, he believed that the Marxian truth was the truth for all men, and the fact that men acted out of motives of greed, hate, and prejudice did not deter him from a belief that governments and institutions, not people, were to blame.

His romanticism prevented him from realizing the most profound truth of all: The victim is a man alone and he will perish or survive according to his own ingenuity or resources. This statement is more true for the victim in America than for those in most other countries. The tendency for the victim to confuse himself with the oppressor in America is very strong. Most black militants are honorable men, far more idealistic and moral than the gentlemen of the N.A.A.C.P. They are committed to ending racism, and they are also committed to a world order in which each man will be free to choose his own destiny. They interpret freedom to mean release from economic oppression, from the burdens of war, and from the excesses of local and national police power.

Dig deeply into their rhetoric and you will unearth a world in which men of all ethnic, racial and religious groups live together in a communal society, share communal affluence, and sup from a communal trough. They prophesy the day of the coming millennium when the existence of the millionaire and the hungry man will have come to an end, when no man will live in a mansion or in a rat infested tenement, when no man will possess more of the earth's bounties than his neighbor. One would imagine that men who hold such thoughts, who see such visions, would have little trouble in recruiting followers, especially among black people for whom dreams and visions are necessary artifacts of life.

The majority of Blacks, however, are more comfortable with the program of the N.A.A.C.P.—with accomodation instead of solution: Let us make our pact with Mephistopheles; on our terms if we can, on his if we must. Every man wants the good things of life, even if to attain these he must sell a pound of flesh or his brother. What is needed, runs the rhetoric of the N.A.A.C.P. spokesmen, is not a new system but a new technician, one who will retune the old system, remove the bugs, and make it work for the majority of the people.

Ivan Karamazov is anathema to the men of the N.A.A.C.P. who have managed to grow fatter in a country where other black men grow angrier. Only the subversive thinks in terms of all or nothing, of saving all men or no men. Nothing in the history of mankind argues the fact that all men can be saved or are worth saving. The race belongs to the swift; the spoils to the victor. We are again with Pavlov and his dogs, and he who seeks to be rewarded must respond to the sound of the right bell. Unlike black militants, the men of the N.A.A.C.P. do not think of replacing the bell with another whose sound will ring true for all men. Among the beneficiaries of the spoils system, they seek to keep it intact with only slight modifications here and there.

A poll in the June 30, 1969 issue of *Newsweek* shows that the majority of black people support the N.A.A.C.P. There is no reason to distrust the polls. Few Blacks see themselves as victims; fewer still are dedicated to dismantling the oppressive American apparatus in total. Men who make five thousand dollars a year, own cars and television sets, and are daily reminded of starvation in Biafra, poverty in Haiti, and apartheid in South Africa, are inclined to support the American system, not destroy it.

How then is Christ to be reconciled with the devil? One must, at least, convince each that the same tyrant rules them both; that the rewards lavished upon one today may be replaced by punishment tomorrow. One does not appeal to morality! Both Christ and the devil have lived in the world too long, have become too sophisticated to accept appeals based upon morality. Therefore, one leaves morality to the ministers and appeals to his comrades on the basis of self interest. Whether my black neighbor likes me as a person or not, my interests and his are the same. The guard who leads me to the concentration camp today, will come back for him tomorrow. If he did not know this before, the events of the last year have done much to educate him.

In the presidential campaign of 1968, Richard Nixon and Spiro T. Agnew dedicated themselves to the task of eliminating crime in the streets and restoring law and order. Undoubtedly this job could have been better performed by George Wallace. Americans, however, are gentle assassins; they would rather starve a man slowly than kill him outright. They elected a sophisticated stand-in for George Wallace as President, and a model closer to the original as Vice President. The turn to the right at the national level was accelerated at the local level. In the mayoral primary elections of 1969, the citizens of Minneapolis nominated a policeman, in Los Angeles they nominated a racist, and in New York they nominated a fascist.

The people, came the message from the White House, are getting fed up with disturbances on the nation's campuses, demonstrations, and crime in the street. Backlash is a phrase created by sensation seeking journalists. The American people are not bigots and racists, are not opposed to Blacks having their rights. Let us bury the Kerner Commission report in the archives along with the Myrdal report; nations are not obligated to accept the findings of men who study them. Sane men, however, do not adhere to the existence of a backlash. Frontlash is a less sensational phrase, but far more accurate a description than the former. What has happened in the country at large is a national regurgitation of long submerged hate. The American cool and poise is eroding under duress. The true national character is emerging in all of its hideousness. Black militants did not create bigotry in America; their actions have not transformed men into fascists overnight. Those who today call for "putting the nigger in his place" did not issue the demand yesterday, for yesterday the nigger was content to stay in his place. This is no longer the case. Beginning with the Black Power movement in 1966, black people initiated a sustained, vigorous drive to eradicate "special places" from the institutions of American life. This meant, in the words of the Black Panther slogan, that white Americans would move over or be moved over. Having grown accustomed to patient, passive, compliant Blacks, the American white middle class, secure in its own place, looked for a hero to return the nation to sanity, to reinstitute the *status quo*, to bring back the "We shall overcome years," to put the nigger back into his place. Heroes are difficult to come by in the American society, and thus, the white middle class was forced to dig back into the past, to manufacture one out of old, discarded timber. In 1969, Richard Nixon became the 37th president of the United States.

Those who elected him president with the belief that he would "put the niggers in their places" are not, it appears, to be disappointed. The school desegregation guidelines and the voting rights bill are being amended in ways calculated to minimize their effectiveness. Anti-poverty programs are being overhauled and many may be scrapped altogether. Black nationalist organizations are being infiltrated, militant black leaders harassed, and, in some cases, jailed. The concentration camps are being made ready and no black man can be sure, that before long, he will not be one of its inmates.

We have come close to racial Armageddon. The scripture applies to men and nations alike: those whom the gods would destroy they first make mad; and America is going through a night of madness. Police departments purchase the heavy machinery of war, shopkeepers arm their help, old ladies in Dearborn, Michigan take target practice, Jewish youths in Brooklyn form defense leagues, citizens in Chicago join vigilante groups, and the children of former victims prepare to make war upon the victims of the present. "And we are here," wrote Matthew Arnold, "as on a darkling plain/ Swept with confused alarms of struggle and flight,/ Where ignorant armies clash by night."

For black people, there are no darkling plains. "Let us not die like hogs," wrote the black poet, Claude McKay, in 1927, and the statement holds true today. We do not want to die at all. Only the insane are eager to exchange life for death. Pain is unbearable, but death is unknowable, and men would rather take their chances with the unbearable than with the unknowable. No, black men do not want to die. But if die we must, then die we will. And we will not die like hogs; we will not be annihilated without taking a fair toll of the oppressor; we will not cleanse this earth with our blood alone; we will not be lined against the wall without offering strong resistance; we will not march to the concentration camps singing "We shall overcome." We will die! And we will die alone. But we will not die passively, on our knees, shouting to some impotent Jesus, "Lord, forgive them for they know not what they do."

I remained beside my father's grave long after the others had gone. I would miss him in the years to come. I seldom obeyed his council, but I was glad that he was around to give it. In fighting so continuously against him, I prepared myself for that much more vicious war with this country. When I left his grave late that night, I still had not cried.

And why should I have cried? The father who died was more fortunate than the son who lived. He lived for fifty-six years, and during this time, his only major disappointment was his son. He lived at a time when hope was still possible, when the chances of an end to the American racial nightmare were a probability, when the world seemed ready to steer clear of nuclear catastrophe. At the time of his death he still clung fervently to his belief that mankind was moving toward creating a society in which the haves and the have-nots would share the world's abundance together. Many times the world disappointed him, but it never gave him cause to be bitter. He saw the rise of new black nations and he saw black men governing those nations. He saw strides taken in the area of human rights in America; and he was convinced that these strides foreshadowed the day when race would have no part in American life. He died as he lived, neither disillusioned nor despondent. In twentieth century America he lived as a romantic and died—a romantic still. In light of such accomplishments, to have cried at his funeral would have been irreligious.

"WE JUST WANTED to march to show our respect," said Renee. "That's all. We didn't want no violence, we just wanted to march . . . because he was a great leader."

She would remember this day, April 4, as the longest of her life. Earlier, she had attended a rally called to protest the racist slurs of a professor at City College. She had implored her fellow students to besiege the members of the state legislature with letters in an attempt to save S.E.E.K.—a college program for young students from the ghetto: "What that professor said about us, you know, it really don't count. I mean, he ain't that important. But them legislators up there [in Albany], if they don't appropriate some money for this program . . . well, you know, like we in trouble."

She had remained at the college after classes to ask non-S.E.E.K. students to join in her protest. Much later, she had attended a concert of African-American dance and music. Here she heard the announcement: "The girl on the stage stopped dancing and she mumbled something. But she had such a thick accent, you know, that we couldn't understand her. Then somebody ran into the auditorium and told us that Dr. King was dead. I didn't believe it . . . no, I still don't."

They left the auditorium in the middle of the concert. Joining hands with almost 200 other students, black and white, Renee marched down Convent Avenue to 125th Street where a worried John Lindsay pleaded with the students to halt. "We stopped," said Renee, "but other people, they had followed us, you know, came along with us. And then they started this."

The "this" was sporadic looting, rock throwing, and the hurling of crudely-made Molotov cocktails. Two men, their arms bulging with loot from a nearby men's store, rushed past, unseen by members of the tactical patrol force who stood four-abreast across the street from the Baby Grand night club. As smoke darkened the sky in the vicinity of Lenox Avenue, fire engines screamed past 125th Street—now barricaded by police vehicles—en route to 126th Street.

Renee shook her head. She was shocked and confused, and a stare of disbelief prevailed in her young eyes. Now and then, the revolving lights of the police vehicles accented the deep lines of her oval-shaped black face. "He didn't approve of violence," she mumbled, "and it ain't right to do this."

There was something pathetic in her words, a sadness in her hurried statements, a look of confusion in her once-bright eyes that told of the tragedy of the moment in a way that no statement from civil rights leaders, no pious declaration from public officials, no "In Memoriam" from gifted writers ever could. Martin Luther King, Jr. had not been her hero. A child of the Black Power Revolution, her heroes were Stokely Carmichael, Malcolm X, and LeRoi Jones. Such men articulated her grievances in a way that Dr. King had not. True enough, she could be momentarily swayed by his eloquence and was subject to moments of ecstasy in anticipation of actual contact with him. Yet, his sonorous tones, his calculated delivery of parenthetical constructions, his many thunderous Miltonic inversions, were the machinery of that evangelical past which she now disparaged. Hers was the world of Camus, of Fanon, of Malraux; and Martin Luther King, Jr. seemed antithetical to all that that world symbolized.

So it was with most of her fellow students. They stood together, huddled in a small circle as if seeking protection from whatever danger, man-made or otherwise, lay concealed in the semi-darkness of this frightful night. They were young men and women for whom Martin Luther King, Jr. had symbolized, not the success of the future, but the failure of the past. Previously they had denounced him in the most vitriolic terms, quoted words from *The Autobiography of Malcolm X* to refute his philosophy, and spoken cynically, though kindly, of his proposed Poor People's March on Washington.

Only their elders had truly kept the faith. They too came to the street corners. Some were drawn by the excitement generated by the events of the day; others, dazed, benumbed, sought solace in the company of those whose misery was akin to their own. Still others, weaving between the groups of people, made their way to the many churches in which Harlem abounds.

Yet, they were united in one common endeavor: the old and the young, those who had kept the faith and those who had renounced all faith; attempting to hold on to some small part of that vision which had been Dr. King's most important asset. The old had believed passionately, fervently, even to the point of idolizing the man who articulated the dream. But the young had believed also. Their present militancy not withstanding, the dream of Martin Luther King, Jr. was more than the dream of their fathers. And no matter the disclaimers they spoke, the postures they assumed, the vehemence with which they rejected American society, the vision of an America free of prejudice, intolerance and injustice was also theirs. And now, tonight, on this most terrible of nights, Dr. King's importance was finally recognized: The most sincere and eloquent spokesman of their cause was dead—assassinated by a white man.

"That's it for me," a neatly dressed young man remarked in passing. "They do something like that to a man like King . . . a man like King."

"Why?" one of the students asked, her eyes red. "Why him?"

"He didn't like no violence," murmured Renee, almost incoherent, "and they killed him anyway."

She began to cry for the first time. She could no longer not believe. Reality was too powerful. Once begun, the tears, a long time in coming, rushed from her eyes as if propelled by a mechanical pump. She stared at the top of a tenement building a few blocks away: "We just wanted to show our respect, you know, to show our respect, because he was a great leader . . ." Another student broke the circle of silence to echo her words, "Yes, a great leader."

She did not hear. She stood unmoving, seeing and yet not seeing, her eyes fixed upon the top of the building. All too soon, the long day had come to an end.

16

CULTURAL HEGEMONY:

THE SOUTHERN WHITE WRITER

AND AMERICAN LETTERS

MOVEMENTS IN LITERARY HISTORY are difficult to discern and the influences which give rise to and sustain them are not easy to trace. The movement from Classicism to Neo-Classicism in seventeenth and eighteenth century English literature cannot be traced to one particular work, although Dryden's *An Essay of Dramatic Poesy*, Samuel Johnson's "Preface to Shakespeare," and Gotthold Lessing's "Laocoon," must be noted. The movement from Neo-Classicism to Romanticism is equally difficult to pinpoint despite the poetry of Thomas Gray, Oliver Goldsmith and William Blake which point to the theories enunciated by Samuel Coleridge in *Biographia Literaria*, William Wordsworth in the preface to *Lyrical Ballads* and Shelley in "A Defense of Poetry."

In America where little of a national literature existed until the latter part of the eighteenth century, any discussion of literary history centers upon the established traditions of Germany, France and England. So great was the foreign influence on American letters that Nathaniel Appleton, Noah Webster, David Ramsay and others demanded a literature of their own. John Trumbill summed up their nationalistic arguments in couplet form:

> This land her Swift and Addison shall view
> The former honors equalled by the new
> Here shall some Shakespear charm the rising age
> And hold in magic chain the listening stage.

David Ramsay demanded a decisive break with the old world. The models to be followed were those of nations that had existed on the shores of the Aegean long ago: "It is hoped that the free government of America will produce poets, orators, critics, and historians equal to the most celebrated of the ancient commonwealths of Greece and Italy." Ramsay's call for an indigenous literature based upon the Greek ideal was not answered until 1830. Cooper's two novels, *The Spy* and *The Last of the Mohicans*, moved the American novel away from the influence of Samuel Richardson and Henry Fielding; Philip Frenau, "the first real poetic voice to be heard in the U.S." broke new grounds in the field of poetry; and the Transcendentalists attempted to lay a philosophical foundation for a national literature. Yet, despite these specific movements, the literary tradition destined to survive the influence of Walt Whitman and William Dean Howells was brought into being by southern writers who, in crossing Aristotle and Plato with Sir Walter Scott, produced a tradition which not only, in Dr. Johnson's words, stood the test of time, but has dominated American cultural thought from 1830 to the present.

The Plantation Movement occurred almost simultaneously with the Transcendental Movement. The latter, dying with Emerson, never reached the status of a tradition, but the former continued to grow and develop. The rise of the one Movement and the demise of the other can be attributed to the fact that the Plantation Movement went back, as Ramsay had suggested, to the Aegean for confirmation of its faith, while the Transcendental Movement went to Germany for its confirmation. Between Emmanuel Kant and Plato lay a world of difference, not only in philosophical approaches but in views of man and society. The voice of Kant calling upon men to be open-minded, to be inquisitive, to approach the complex problems of men in humanitarian terms, fell on deaf ears in a nation where prejudice, dogmatism, and simplistic approaches to problems, human and social, were and still are the norm. Given the choice between Platonic idealism and Kantian transcendentalism, the South chose to ally itself with the Greek mind and thus became the embodiment of the American myth.

The earliest proponent of this myth was the statesman-philosopher, John C. Calhoun; and American cultural thought is more indebted to Calhoun than critics and teachers care to admit. In defending the plantation system, Calhoun championed a republic modeled on the Greek ideal, one with a strong class structure. He devoted himself, according to Parrington, "to set class economics above abstract humanitarianism . . . He undid for the plantation South the work of his old master [Jefferson]. Speaking in the name of democracy, he attacked the foundations on which the democratic movement in America had rested, substituting for its libertarian and equalitarian doctrines conceptions wholly alien and antagonistic to western democracy, wholly Greek in their underlying spirit."

With Calhoun, the defense of the plantation system passed from Virginia to South Carolina. Virginia, inoculated with the philosophy of Thomas Jefferson, and with her plantation system working at peak performance, had settled down to the complacency of an affluent Greek city-state. With abolitionism on the rise in the North, the *Appeal* of the black writer, David Walker, calling for slave insurrections flooding the South, and the plantation system under daily attack, Calhoun appears to present the rationale for what Thomas Nelson Page called "the purest sweetest life ever lived."

In "A Disquisition on Government," Calhoun declared: ". . . it is a great and dangerous error to suppose that all people are equally entitled to liberty. It is a reward to be earned not a blessing to be gratuitously lavished on all alike—a reward reserved for the intelligent, the patriotic, the virtuous and deserving—and not a boon to be bestowed on a people too ignorant, degraded and vicious, to be capable either of appreciating or of enjoying it . . . Nor is it any disparagement to liberty that such is and ought to be the case. On the contrary, its greatest praise—its proudest distinction is, that an all-wise providence has reserved it, as the noblest and highest reward for the development of our faculties, moral and intellectual." Having carried us thus far in pursuit of the Greek ideal, having paid his debt to the early Plato of *The Republic*, Calhoun turns to invoke the spirit of the later Plato whose last dialogue, *The Laws*, is a treatise on despotism: "A reward more appropriate than liberty could not be conferred on the deserving—nor punishment inflicted on the undeserving more just, than to be subject to lawless and despotic rule."

For an accurate summation of Calhoun's thought on this point, one must turn to Vernon Parrington: "Democracy is possible only in a society that recognizes inequality as a law of nature, but in which the virtuous and capable enter into a voluntary co-partnership for the common good, accepting wardship of the incompetent in the interests of society. This was the Greek ideal and this ideal had created Greek civilization."

In "Remarks on the States Rights Resolutions in Regard to Abolition," Calhoun describes the new Republic: ". . . The southern states are an aggregate, in fact, of communities, not of individuals. Every plantation is a little community, with the master at its head, who concentrates in himself the united interests of capital and labor, of which he is the common representative. These small communities aggregated make the State in all, whose action, labor, and capital is equally represented and perfectly harmonized. Hence the harmony, the union, the stability of that section which is rarely disturbed, except through the action of this government."

John Pendleton Kennedy, William Alexander Caruthers, and Nathaniel Beverley Tucker, among the South's earliest literary lights, accepted the Calhoun sociological doctrine totally and lent their talents to extolling the virtues of the plantation system. Contrary to popular belief, their major efforts were not spent in defending the institution of slavery but in praising the virtue of the concept on which the plantation system rested. The defense of slavery by Calhoun and Albert Taylor Bledsoe in the social, political and theological realm was not undertaken in earnest by poets and writers until after the publication of *Uncle Tom's Cabin* in 1852. Until then, the men of letters had been content with propagandizing the virtues of the Greek ideal.

The southern mind was attracted to this ideal partly because of the justification for slavery offered by the world's first "democracy"; it was not attracted by what Matthew Arnold called the humane principles handed down from the Aegean—principles which distinguished man as the center of the universe. To the southern mind, historically incapable of dealing with complexity, and seeking a stable, ordered society free from the disruption occasioned by the intrusion of enlightened ideas, Greece offered a model of the agrarian society, Athens, a universe where each man, awarded his place in society, lived by a set of norms which defined his daily existence and by extension defined him.

Plato's *The Republic* and Aristotle's *Politics,* not the King James version of the Bible, are the ancient tracts from which the southerners gleaned their theology. Central to each of these works is the idea of the planned society in which men and women function as a unit—a world of superiors and inferiors, each cognizant of his particular niche in the social, political, and cultural hierarchy. Having laid the sociological and political basis for such a utopia, John C. Calhoun turned his attention to the coming break between North and South and left the task of singing its glories, of recording it in verse, prose and song to poets and novelists. When these "legislators of the world," as Shelley called them, took up their pens to describe Calhoun's world, the plantation system became the model for the plantation school of writers who originated a tradition destined to survive for over two hundred years.

In this literature one finds, almost everywhere the dramatization of the perfect society whose closest analogue is Lovejoy's theory of the "Great Chain of Being." At the apex of the chain was the master, God's vice-regent on earth, Solon and Christ combined, bold, generous and philanthropic, bending man and beast to his will with cajolery if possible, with the whip if necessary. The lesser plantation owner, whose wealth calculated in terms of number of slaves, was insufficient to grant him top status, was next. Next came the farmer, and following him were the peasants, the poor whites who, due to lack of ingenuity, were incapable of surviving in a Darwinian world. At the bottom were the slaves upon whose shoulders the task of maintaining the plantation system rested. They were the inferior element, and a modern day supporter of the plantation system, John Gould Fletcher, has justified their existence at the lower rung of the hierarchy: "The inferior, whether in life or in education, should exist only for the sake of the superior. We feed and clothe and exercise our bodies, for example, in order to be able to do something with our minds. We employ our minds in order to achieve character, to become the balanced personalities, the 'superior men' of Confucius' text, the 'Gentlemen' of the old south."

The "superior men of Confucius' text" remain the heroes of plantation literature. Their most important characteristics are devotion to region, duty and loved ones. The loved ones are often fair damsels, ladies whose material possessions are fans, musical boxes, billets-doux and perfumed handkerchiefs. In addition to Plato and Aristotle, the influence of Sir Walter Scott, Samuel Richardson and Alexander Pope is apparent everywhere. The idyllic utopia, the paradise on earth, is re-created in poetry and fiction with the authenticity vouchsafed it by the rhetoric of John C. Calhoun.

Calhoun died in 1850, two years before the plantation tradition came under assault from Harriet Beecher Stowe. Although based upon slavery, one must not think of the plantation system and the institution of slavery as one and the same. In so doing, critics have attributed motives to Harriet Beecher Stowe which she did not entertain. Mrs. Stowe had no intention of "starting the big war," nor did she seek to do away with the slave system. Unlike her father, Lyman Beecher, and her brother, Henry, Mrs. Stowe was not an abolitionist. What bothered her was not slavery but the immorality of the institution which offended her Quaker sensitivity and led her, without realizing it, to explode the myth the plantation system rested upon.

The society of southern mythology could be justified by its apologists only if it rested on a high plane of morality. Inferiors had to be treated humanely or proved deserving of punishment then inflicted upon them by loving masters, pushed beyond the limits of patience. Rewarding instead of abusing those who "stayed in their places" was an unwritten law of the ideal republic which, when violated, introduced chaos into the system. No slave was more conscious of his position than Tom, none accepted so readily the "place" to which providence and ill fortune had doomed him, and none was more obedient, loving or submissive.

Tom's treatment at the hands of Simon Legree, who, as Edmund Wilson points out, is the plantation owner, a yankee, not an overseer and a southerner as most people have been led to believe, does irreparable injury to the ideal which southern writers had been propagating and reveals the plantation system to have been modeled less upon Plato and Aristotle than upon Epicurus and Heraclitus. He is not the victim of "the most pernicious institution known to man," but the victim of an imperfect social order, one which fails to live up to its promise. Whatever others might make of *Uncle Tom's Cabin* for abolitionist ends, Mrs. Stowe would have settled for a world in which the justice and humanity espoused by southern writers was an actuality; one in which an "inferior" like Tom who never violates the norms of his condition is accorded due treatment for loyalty, devotion and piety.

Southern writers have always been aware of the underlying thesis of Mrs. Stowe's novel. Their counter-attack was not ostensibly based upon a defense of slavery but upon a defense of the plantation system. They went to great lengths to prove that the Simon Legrees were anomolies, and that the black Toms of the South fared better than the white Toms of the North. The tenacious zeal displayed in articulating the virtues of Calhoun's "near perfect society" was now marshalled in defense of it.

Less than one year after the publication of *Uncle Tom's Cabin*, William John Grayson, who with George Fitzhugh formed a two-man truth squad dedicated to correcting the falsehoods of Mrs. Stowe, used the heroic couplet as the medium for his rebuttal. Black slaves in the South, he argued in "The Hireling and the Slave," fare far better than the northern poor; and after cataloguing the abuses of the poor in the North, he contrasts their plight with that of the slaves in the South:

> If bound to daily labor while he lives,
> His the daily bread that labor gives:
> Guarded from want, from beggary secure,
> He never feels what hireling crowds endure,
> Nor knows like them, in hopeless want to crave,
> For wife and child, the comforts of the slave,
> Or the sad thought that, when about to die
> He leaves them to the cold world's charity
> And sees them slowly seek the poor-house door—
> The last, vile, hated refuge of the poor.

George Fitzhugh, choosing to mount his defense in prose, based his argument in *Cannibals All/or Slaves Without Masters*, on the same theme. In "Slavery—Its Effects on the Free," he meets the moral argument posed by Mrs. Stowe without retreating one step from the Greek ideal: "Now at first view it [slavery] elevates . . . whites; for it makes them not the bottom of society, as at the North—not the menials, the hired day laborers, the work scavengers and scullions—but privileged citizens, like Greek and Roman citizens, with a numerous class far beneath them." And reminiscent of Grayson, Fitzhugh concludes: "Our slaves till the land, do the coarse and hard labor on our roads and canals, sweep our streets, cook our food, brush our boots, wait on our tables, hold our horses, do all hard work, and fill all menial offices. Your freemen at the North do the same work and fill the same offices. The only difference is, we love our slaves, and are ready to defend, assist and protect them. . . ."

Such gallant defenses proved of no avail against the juggernaut now poised to move in the North. Three years after Fitzhugh's *Cannibals All*, "the irrepressible conflict" erupted into a violent conflagration in which men like William Tecumseh Sherman, riding the whirlwind of the apocalypse, burned to ashes the physical props on which had rested the literature of the South. When chaos came, when peace and tranquility was disrupted, all that would survive of the Greek ideal was a record of what men believed had once existed.

The writers after Reconstruction—Thomas Nelson Page, Thomas Dixon and Joel Chandler Harris—brooded over the past, attempted to resurrect it in fiction and poetry, to create the Garden of Eden once again. The paradise lost haunted them all of their lives, and they died, pitiable old men, clinging to the dream of ancient Greece which once flowered anew on American soil. The dream would not die with them. They lived during the years of "the bloody shirt" when every northern politician singled out the South as villain, when John Brown replaced Davy Crockett as the national hero, and when the best literary talents of the North were celebrating the virtues of "old New England."

When the days of northern vindictiveness were over, when the railroad men discovered new routes in the South, when the

Supreme Court had struck down the last of the Reconstruction legislation, and when president Hayes had withdrawn the last troops from the South, other men, dreaming the dreams of Post-Reconstruction writers, awakened to ask with Fletcher: "How can we preserve what little is now left to us of the traditions of leisure, of culture, of intellectual tolerance and sane kindliness, which are all that our fathers had to give us as a legacy from the past that was broken in the civil war?"

No longer the interpreter of the system or its defender, the task for the southern writer was now "to forge from the smithy of his soul the uncreated conscious of the race." He set out at first to justify the ways of Calhoun to his southern brethren; and he was oblivious of the fact, until much later, that his appeal was listened to and applauded by those in the ranks of the enemy. Despite Parrington's attempt to subordinate the influence of the Plantation School to that of the Trascendentalists and the Realists, it has with its simplistic view of man and the world remained dominant in American literature.

Men like Fletcher, better educated and more sophisticated than their predecessors, discovered Matthew Arnold's truth—that great creative epochs demand great ideas to propel them into being and that to accomplish this task, an era of literary criticism is necessary. Such men, apostles of a modern romanticism who refused to believe that the southern Athens was gone beyond recall, set out to seize the reins of literary criticism in America, to force it into new and different channels and to posit a romanticism far less humane than that which they set out to destroy.

The New Critics appeared at a time when complexity was the norm in American life. In the late twenties and early thirties, the society was undergoing spasms from forces as varied as race riots and industrial expansion. The influence and power of the priest had been dissipated; the politician had lost favor through perversion of his art. The social institutions everywhere seemed incapable of confronting the complexity of life in the twentieth century. There was an overwhelming moral and social void and, like the men of the middle ages, the men of twentieth century America turned to the university, calling on it to wage war in the interests of progress, to construct the formulas by which a nation might rise or fall.

Men who held such naive faith in the universities learned the lesson that young college students are learning today: The most reactionary institution in American society is the university, and the last place that one will find enlightenment, morality or redemption is within its ivy-covered walls. Nowhere outside of the university is the southern myth of the simplistic universe more pervasive, nowhere the aristocratic ideal held so dear, nowhere the vision of Calhoun clung to so tenaciously, and nowhere are the Greeks treated with more regard as the accurate prophets of man's existence. The American university has not changed essentially since the founding of Harvard College in 1636. Its purpose then as now was "to provide for young gentlemen a body of knowledge that would assure entrance into a community of educated leaders."

Toward these ends the university channeled its energy and its resources. Obsessed with the idea of establishing an educational aristocracy, the men of the university hastened to defend the validity of tradition, despite the precarious position upon which it rested. Despite the efforts of a few professors—outcasts among their peers—the tracts, books and articles supporting the institution of slavery, and perpetuating the nonsense of the black man's inferiority poured out of universities, North as well as South. For a while the historians were the chief villains in this comedy of errors, but soon the torch was passed on to the teachers of literature.

The English departments were ready for the New Critics who, in the latter part of the 1920's began to remodel literary criticism in their own agrarian (read plantation) image. They left the southern universities, took up residence at the Universities in the North, and proceeded to construct a republic in letters based upon the social republic which they outlined in *I'll Take My Stand*.

Sometimes called "the Bible of agrarianism," *I'll Take My Stand* is a racist, fascist document, equalled in the twentieth century only by Hitler's *Mein Kampf*. Among its contributors are men whose names are legend in the field of American literary criticism. Included are articles by Donald Davidson who in 1954 "became chairman of the Tennessee Federation for Constitutional Government," a right wing organization "formed to oppose desegregation on the principle of states rights;" Allen Tate whose introduction to *Libretto for the Republic of Liberia* by Melvin B. Tolson surpasses William Dean Howells' "Preface" to *The Complete Works of Paul Laurence Dunbar* in racial bigotry and arrogant, Aryan superiority; and Robert Penn Warren who has denounced his contribution to *I'll Take My Stand*, admitting that "it was written in support of segregation." However, in his conclusion to *Who Speaks for the Negro?*, published in 1965, Warren evidences how far along the road to rehabilitation he has travelled, and shows to be not very far at all.

In *I'll Take My Stand*, the major thesis is a reiteration of the social thesis propounded by Calhoun in the 1830's. We are called to a rebirth of the republic of Athens, and asked to reconstruct the society formed along class lines which existed in the South before the coming modern evils, progress and industrialism, intervened. We are asked to follow the agrarians back to the time when ". . . the even-poised and leisurely life of the Greeks, their oratory, their philosophy, their art . . . appealed to the South. The Greek tradition became partly grafted upon the Anglo-Saxon and Scotch tradition of life."

"The remarkable society" of the old South (Allen Tate's terminology) was not defeated in the civil war. Actual defeat threatens it now. The modern invaders are a varied assortment of incompatible elements: factories, railroads, bureaucrats and civil rights agitators. These seek to change the simplistic life of a simple people, to destroy the romantic past born of rich soil, cultured old gentlemen and docile slaves. Against this modern aggression, the twelve writers take their stand, prepared to defend "a special notion of tradition—a notion that tradition is not simply a fact but a fact that must be constantly defended."

For these twentieth century southern writers, tradition means what it meant for the plantation writers of the eighteenth and nineteenth centuries: a theory of society which goes back to the founding fathers of the old South, one based on the doctrines of

Plato and Aristotle, a tradition in which the great chain of being stands as the metaphor of man's hopes and strivings, where aristocrat, farmer, and especially the black man know their places. "In the past," writes Robert Penn Warren, "the Southern Negro has always been a creature of the small town and farm. That is where he still chiefly belongs by temperament and capacity; there he has less the character of a 'problem' and more the status of a human being who is likely to find in agricultural and domestic pursuits the happiness that his good nature and easy ways incline him to as an ordinary function of his being."

How then, Allen Tate asks, can this tradition which survives in southern letters be resurrected again in actuality? His answer is definitive: "The answer is by violence . . . Since he [the southerner] cannot bore from within, he has left the sole alternative of boring from without. This method is political, active, and in the nature of the case, violent and revolutionary. Reaction is the most radical of programs; it aims at cutting away the overgrowth and getting back to the roots."

Like the novels of Thomas Dixon which sanctioned the activities of the Ku Klux Klan when other men believed that tradition should be defended to the death, the contributors to *I'll Take My Stand* provided the rationale for the violence enacted against Arthurine Lucy and James Meredith, for the murders of Emmett Till, Jimmy Lee Jackson and Medgar Evers, for the bombing of five black children in a Birmingham church, and for the elevation of the Bull Connors and George Wallaces to a national eminence approaching sainthood.

Tate and his fellow southerners misjudged the American temper. The book was written as a defense of the southern way of life and directed at a supposedly hostile audience in the rest of the nation. However, Americans, to paraphrase William Blake, were not only of the Devil's party, but with the exception of a few misguided liberals, recognized their close affiliation. America is most southern in her inclination to favor Aristotle over Immanuel Kant, to opt for the simplistic life instead of the complex one, and to believe as passionately in the concept of the great chain of being as the most rabid southern aristocrat. The true character of white America was difficult to analyze during the period of continual wars and migration from country to city and from city to suburbs.

The case is quite different today. Supplied with a life of affluence and leisure surpassed in American history only by the plantation owner and the managerial capitalist, Americans today look forward to peace, comfort and security. Few would be shocked by the philosophy displayed in *I'll Take My Stand;* a great many would accept these fascist myths of the thirties as the truths for the seventies. The republic imagined in writing stands a chance today of being established in fact by the administration of Richard Nixon whose architects seem determined to transform America into a shadow image of the plantation system of yesteryear.

The nation was thirty years late in recognizing its true character. However, the university principles fell sway to the sophistry of the agrarians in less than two years. The initial assault was made on the English departments. Guardians of the national taste, these men of letters determine what cultured Americans will or will not read, what work of art deserves or does not deserve the National Book Award or the Pulitzer Prize, what writer will or will not receive a fellowship to work in leisure or a seat at a renowned university. The control of the nation's cultural apparatus rests in the hands of English professors and critics who, more often than not, peer out upon the American society with a condescension usually reserved for idiots and half-wits.

Such men welcomed the attempt of the New Critics to establish an aristocracy in American letters equal to that which they envisioned in the social sphere. The days of Hyppolyte Taine and Charles Augustin Sainte-Beuve were no more. Literature which dealt with man in terms of "race, moment and milieu," which considered the life of the author as important as the work itself, which argued that literature should not only mean but have a moral function as well, was denounced as irrelevant in a society where the artist sought not the elevation of mankind but the cultivation of his art.

A poem or a novel, like a well wrought urn, was an "autotelic structure," governed by inner rules and conforming to verbal structures which only the chosen few could analyze or interpret. The function of the writer was not, as Henry Fielding had believed, to instruct but to produce masterpieces which would satisfy the aesthetic tastes of the cultured elite—tastes conditioned by four years of English courses "in the best colleges and universities."

If America is to again become the legendary Athens, a literature which serves the demands of the aristocracy is a necessity. Still dreaming of the past, still enamored of the theories of the utopian society propounded by J. C. Calhoun, the agrarians seized upon the psychological criticism of I. A. Richards, the ambiguous criticism of T. S. Eliot, imbued it with their own biases and formulated a theory of art for art's sake with the concomitant denial of the democratic spirit and disdain for the masses.

When the English departments accepted the "ars poetica" of the Southern Agrarians, they chose to deal with literature in terms applicable to the plastic arts; moreover, they substantiated the southern myth and gave authenticity to a society constructed along class lines. Their hypnotic attraction to the Greek ideal led them to accept the agrarian formula of a master class for whose personal comfort a literature was created. In so doing, they championed the worst of the plantation tradition and preceded the rest of the nation in succumbing to the philosophy of the descendants of Calhoun.

Nowhere is the influence of the plantation tradition more pronounced than in literature which deals with Blacks. Afro-Americans are the descendants of those whose presence in America made the plantation system possible; and the literary tradition based upon it owes as much to their presence as to the works of Plato and Sir Walter Scott.

Assigned the lowest positions on the great chain of being. Blacks, in attempting to extricate themselves, have evoked repercussions from white Americans in social, political, economic, and cultural areas. After the Emancipation Proclamation, in order to preserve the legacy left by the Plantation School of writers, white writers and critics instituted cultural slavery to replace the chattel slavery ended by the guns of war.

In 1925, in the preface to *The New Negro*, Alain Locke noted the cultural servitude under which Blacks labored and attributed this to the efforts of teachers and critics to deal with them in stereotypic terms. Locke's solution was to have the Negro speak for himself. However, Americans turned to white oracles. They preferred to listen to voices more attuned to their own, to those who spoke of peace and tranquility instead of war, who sought to assuage their fears with romance and make believe instead of presenting the true story of America in all of its "hideous fullness."

No two oracles were more soothing in this respect than William Faulkner and William Styron. Nowhere in American literature does the plantation tradition reach greater heights than in the portraits of black characters drawn by these writers. White critics of William Faulkner and their black fellow travellers—Ralph Ellison and Albert Murray are the best known—have praised him for his "realistic portrayal of Negro people." However, his Negro characters, whose function is to satisfy the demand of white Americans for racial peace, are remnants of the plantation tradition.

Dilsey of *The Sound and the Fury* is one example. Like the "mammies" of Paul Laurence Dunbar's *Strength of Gideon,* her literary lineage goes back to Thomas Nelson Page: she attempts to hold the white family together, she is the foundation of a dying institution, and, while suffering insult and abuse, she survives by virtue of patience and submissiveness. The Greek ideal is safe with the Dilseys of the earth. Knowing and accepting their places, they face each tomorrow with a Bible under their arms, not with Molotov cocktails under their skirts. They are, to be sure, far different from the Harriet Tubmans and Sojourner Truths of actual American history.

Dilsey is the prototype of the good nigger, the darling of the earlier followers of the plantation tradition. No threat to the institution of slavery, she accepts her position in the hierarchy as having been ordained by God, and she will never bring chaos into the republic. Faulkner displayed great enthusiasm for the Dilseys of the race who became his metaphor for those whom other Blacks should emulate: "The Negro . . . must learn to cease forever thinking like a Negro and acting like a Negro . . . What he must learn are the hard things—self restraint, honesty, dependability, purity; to act not even as well as just any white man, but to act as well as the best of white men."

No Black should emulate Joe Christmas of *Light in August*. One cannot exist in Faulkner's world half white or half black, and the mulatto, a man with no discernible place, is doomed to an ignominious existence and a tragic end.

Without roots in either black society or white, he is an outcast. He is the tragic mulatto of the plantation tradition who comes to prominence after the Civil War. The bad nigger of southern fiction, he survives in Faulkner as a reminder of the evils of miscegenation—that act for which J. C. Calhoun made no provisions and which may eventually bring about the destruction of the existing social order.

A reassurance and a warning, this is the sum total of Faulkner's contribution to American letters; and Americans are more likely to remember the reassurance (Dilsey) than the warning (Joe Christmas). This is due, in part, to *The Confessions of Nat Turner*, by William Styron. Coming in the midst of the Black Revolution, Styron's novel reassures white Americans who had begun to believe that Malcolm X, Stokely Carmichael and H. Rap Brown posed a threat to the maintenance of the great society. These men who chose the philosophy of Sparta over that of Athens were, it was believed, prepared to lead the Spartan hordes from the ghettoes on an adventure designed to destroy the caste and class sytem upon which the republic stands.

Nat Turner was thrust upon the national consciousness to remind white Americans that, historically, all black revolutionaries have had Achilles heels. What they desire in actuality is not the master's life, but his daughter, and they are so confused about their relationship vis-à-vis white society that any determined assault upon white America, if it comes at all, is many years distant. Therefore these modern day Nat Turners pose no real threat, for not only are they half men, but they are sexually disturbed as well, seeking to wage war not in the streets or behind the barricades but in the bedrooms of white women.

Nat Turner in the hands of Richard Wright, LeRoi Jones or John Williams would have been altogether different. And those who condemn Styron for his portrait, who demand that he portray Nat Turner with some semblance of reality, demand the impossible. To demand a realistic portrayal of Blacks by whites is to demand the impossible; for whites are neither mentally nor culturally equipped for the task. The plantation sentiments are too strong in white America, the influence of the New Critics too pervasive. Their approach to black people can only travel the gamut from crude distortion to condescension occasioned by racism either unconscious or overt.

This is readily apparent in the area of literary criticism. Theodore Gross, the new Robert Bone of Black literature, lauds Joel Chandler Harris for being "able to share the fears, laughter, and anger of the Negro; he contributed the most popular Negro characters to American fiction—Uncle Remus, Balam, Ananias, and Mingo." Richard Wright, according to the same critic, when writing of his life and experiences in *Black Boy*, is found to depict "mundane actualities."

The assumptions upon which Gross' critical thesis rests are stated in his essay, *Our Mutual Estates*: whites, he argues, due to their training in "America's best universities," are better equipped to deal with Black literature than Blacks. His thesis is supported by, among others, Fred Ehrenfeld who, in reviewing the anthology, *How We Live: Contemporary Life in Contemporary Fiction*, finds that, "Of the seven selections devoted to the Negro, two are by Jews and one by a southern white writer. The editor feels the need to justify this by contending that there are few good black writers."

These are the disciples of the New Critics, the academic architects of a new aristocracy, and their arguments are cogently summed up by Seldman Rodman in a review of Melvin Tolson's *Libretto for the Republic of Liberia*. After noting that Black literature has been "praised for its moral intentions and excused for its formal shortcomings," Rodman writes ". . . most of this poetry has been second rate, and critics, partaking of the general responsibility for the Negro's unreadiness to take the 'Negro Problem' in his stride, have hesitated to say so. The Negro poet's attitude of resigned pathos was followed by one of tragic aggressiveness, and both, as Allen Tate says in his preface to 'Libretto for the Republic of Liberia' limited him 'to a provincial mediocrity in which feelings about one's difficulties become more important than poetry itself.' "

To end with a quotation from the dean of southern literary criticism is a measure of the extent of the influence of the southern writer upon American letters; and it is no misstatement to say that American culture today is little more than a fiefdom of southerners who exercise more despotic control over the national literature than their forefathers exercised over their plantations. Against this cultural dominance stands a small band of black intellectuals and writers whose history has been one of continual struggle against the Greek ideal. More Kantian than Aristotelian, their vision is grounded in the ideals of democracy; they believe in art for people's sake, as one of their most respected poets, Don L. Lee, has so aptly put it; and they argue for cultural freedom as opposed to cultural imperialism.

Nothing could be farther from the minds of these Black intellectuals than saving America from despotism of any kind; yet, in propounding the thesis of a Black Aesthetic, they offer an instrument as potent as that of the early American writers who sought to break the domination of their culture by Frenchmen, Englishmen, and Germans. In freeing American letters from southern tyranny, in advocating critical rules opposed to the anti-humanistic ones of the disciples of the New Critics, in postulating a literature which functions in the interest of all mankind, they may bring about a revolution in American letters designed to usher in a new freedom for all writers—white and black alike.

17

SEPARATE,

NOT MUTUAL ESTATES

"For I was born, far from my native clime,
Under the white man's menace, out of time."
—CLAUDE McKAY

"OF ALL THE VOLUMINOUS LITERATURE on the Negro," wrote Alain
Locke in the foreword to the anthology *The New Negro* (1925),
"so much is mere external view and commentary that we may
warrantably say that nine-tenths of it is about the Negro rather
than of him. . . ." Professor Locke was too kind a critic to
specify that much of this "voluminous literature" was written not
by Blacks, but by whites. Between the year of the publication of
Clotel (1853), the first novel by a Black writer by William Wells
Brown; and the year of *The Survey Graphic* (1925) edition
which supplied most of the material for *The New Negro*, over
one hundred and fifty volumes—primarily criticism—were published by whites about Blacks.

The most offensive of these publications came not from the
pens of sentimentalists like Thomas Nelson Page or overt bigots
like Thomas Dixon, but, for the most part, from well-educated,
competent, academic scholars. A sample list of titles illustrates
their critical temperament: *The Negro: A Beast in the Image of
God, The Color Line: A Brief in Behalf of the Unborn, The
Negro, a Menace to Civilization.* The dean of these academic
scholars was John Burgess who declared from his chair at Colum-
bia University in *Reconstruction and the Constitution:* "A black
skin means membership in a race of men which has never of itself
succeeded in subjecting passion to reason, has never, therefore,

186

created any civilization of any kind. There is something natural in the subordination of an inferior race to a superior race, even to the point of enslavement of the inferior race. . . . It is the white man's duty and his right to hold the reins of political power in his own hands for the civilization of the world and the welfare of mankind."

The social critics were joined by literary critics (also educated in "our best universities") who attacked the works of Black writers from a more benevolent, though equally abusive, perspective. "It appears to me now," declared William Dean Howells, one of America's few literary dictators, "that there is a precious difference of temperament between the two races which it would be a great pity ever to lose, and that this is best preserved and most charmingly suggested by Mr. Dunbar [Paul Laurence Dunbar] in those pieces of his where he studies the moods and traits of his own race in its accents of our English . . . he reveals in these a finely ironic perception of the Negro's limitations. . . ."

This "damning with faint praise" was not peculiar to Howells alone. In conversation with James Weldon Johnson, H. L. Mencken proved himself also a master of the art. In his autobiography, *Along This Way*, Johnson notes that: "He [Mencken] declared that Negro writers in writing about their race made a mistake when they indulged in pleas for justice and mercy . . . when they based their unjust treatment on the Christian or moral ethical code. . . ." And, with that characteristic arrogance of white critics from Howells to Theodore Gross, Mencken vouchsafed this directive: "What they should do is to single out the strong points of the race and emphasize them over and over."

The fatherly advice of Mencken, the feigned liberal criticism of Howells, and the overt, biased appraisal of Burgess spring from the same source—a contempt for Black people which, despite having been "educated in our best universities," sorely affected the judgment of these critics. For each believed that Black people were indeed descendants of Ham who, like Benedict Spinoza, were to be accursed by day and night, in lying down and getting up, in going out and coming in. These accursed people, therefore, were the stanchions of an idyllic utopia ruled over by a race of Aryan superiors. The logical conclusion to this premise is evident: the creations of such people, whether material or intellectual, are to be censured as inferior and unimportant in an America of superior cultural, intellectual, and artistic attainment.

These *a priori* assumptions made by men who, like Kyo in *Man's Fate*, must be the guardians of the destinies of other men as well as their own, are remnants of that curious duplicity of American social life born in slavery. Thomas Jefferson's encomiums on the rights of man and the equalitarian society were negated by the physical presence of the many slaves who maintained his Monticello home. William Lloyd Garrison who declared his refusal to equivocate on the issue of slavery, nevertheless broke with Frederick Douglass, who had taken the radical position of John Brown, opting for revolution instead of "moral suasion."

Such duplicity evidences the "plantation mentality" codified in the writings of Dixon and Page and expropriated, almost *in toto*, by white critics today. In the modern version of the plantation credo, Black people are neither mysterious nor inscrutable; they are far from being wearers of the mask, as Dunbar asserts, or invisible men, as Ellison describes. At most, they are the wards of western civilization; a simple folk whose ideas are primitive, whose morals are perverse, and whose manners are unrefined. Any white critic is therefore capable of interpreting the ways of such people to Black and white alike. ("I have told you my truth," shouted Nietzsche's Zarathustra, "and now you may tell me yours." However, white critics have assumed that their truths about Blacks are definitive.)

This arrogance, close to what George Meredith called "self importance born of excessive hubris," is nowhere more evident today than on the college campuses of America. The oracle has been shifted from Delphi to the classrooms of America's largest universities—though, the young Socrates who journeys here for enlightenment in the area of Black studies will find that the mistress of the oracle has fled, her seat now occupied by decrepit gnomes who dispense not wisdom, but falsehoods, moral platitudes, and nonsensical clichés.

Here, upon this Olympian tower, like Washington Irving's "headless horseman," the spirits of Howells, Mencken, and Burgess ride roughshod over the Black Ichabods. And here, too, sits

Shelley's "winged hound" feeding on the heart of the prostrate Black Prometheus, while the gnomish gods formulate those theories and ideas by which Black people might "live and die." Steadily, increasingly, the heralds come from Olympus via periodicals and publishing houses to those mortals who consider the new gods —distinct from the old gods, Dryden, Pope, and Johnson—to be the "fountainhead of all wisdom and judgment."

There is this, however, about the new Olympians: their flaws are even more pronounced than those of the mortals whom they purport to instruct. In a universe where racism is so all pervasive, contempt for Blacks so definitive, and the need of white liberals to serve as father figures so obsessive, the rulers of Olympus share the racist infection of the society at large with all its inherent biases and prejudices.

Nowhere is this more pronounced than in literary criticism, and nowhere shown more explicitly than in a recent article, "Mutual Estates," written by Theodore Gross and published in the winter edition of *Antioch Review*. Like most white critics, Gross pretends to view the works of Black writers from an objective vantage point, believing in the myth perpetuated by "The New Critics" of the nineteen twenties that a critic is capable of bringing to the work of art a judgment free of the influence of the political and social climate of his time. Such an assumption leads Gross to inveigh against W.E.B. DuBois, James Weldon Johnson, Alain Locke, and Sterling Brown; competent critics whose only fault is that they "have been Negro social leaders." Believing that the two must be mutually exclusive, Gross exclaims, "In their desire to preserve the artifacts of a cultural past they have often acted as benevolent censors of their creative contemporaries."

Gross' thesis has been stated more honestly, forcefully, and explicitly before. In an article on two Black critics, Pearl Thomas and Carolyn Reese, in *The Teachers College Record* (1967), Robert Bone avows: "Miss Thomas is a birthright critic, miraculously schooled in Negro literature by virtue of her race alone," while Miss Reese, "cannot deal with Negro poetry because at bottom she has failed to acquire the necessary skills."

However, the salient characteristic of literary criticism from Sainte-Beuve to T. S. Eliot has been that all criticism begins from a subjective point of view; from—to use Alexander Pope's oftmisinterpreted word—taste, a starting point conditioned by the social, cultural, and political environment. For this reason, Aristotle chose a play by his countryman, Sophocles, to formulate a theory of tragedy; Dr. Johnson followed suit in expanding that theory; and Wordsworth, evaluating the poetry of his eighteenth century predecessors, initiated the dialogue on poetic language begun in the "Preface" to *Lyrical Ballads*.

That each critic reacts to the social, cultural, and political mores of his time should be no surprise to scholars and, indeed, would not be if the implications for white American critics were not so damning. Now that the critic is forced to deal with the lives of a people immune to analysis from the Olympian tower, and disdaining to acquire "the necessary skills" through empirical investigation, he is either relegated to the staid, narrow criticism of the New Critics, or forced to hand down dicta which have no foundation in actuality.

White critics are forced to deal with Black literature in terms postulated by Archibald MacLeish, adopting completely the assertion that literature "should not mean but be." The literary work of art is thus transformed into artifact, and the written word subjected to the type of critical analysis forwarded by the Bell-Fry school in painting, where art as object is judged solely in terms of form, technique, and aesthetic structure. To be sure, the Bell-Fry theory of criticism when applied to literature, mandates being "educated in our best universities" and, were it possible to apply, would obliterate the prejudice which each critic brings to a literary work; thereby allowing white critics to deal with Black literature through the "back door" approach.

Gross tells us: "Wherever Americans meet, the subject is race and, one suspects, not only because of the unsettling practical problems aroused by the subject but because it threatens the very preconceptions that Americans have about their own morality." If this is true—and it is no more true today than in the days of Burgess, Howells, and Mencken—then no aspect of American life can be insulated from the climate produced by such discussion; and no American can bring pure objectivity to any endeavor undertaken by Black people. It is very important to hold fast to this with all candor: white critics are white first, and the term critic is easily discarded where Black literature is concerned. For in a society in which racism is so all pervasive, the present day critic, like his counterpart of yesteryear, is unlikely to remain untainted.

Robert Bone, for example, proves incapable of discarding the robes of the past. With the arrogance of a Howells, he proposes to instruct Black writers not only on literary technique, but also on their moral responsibility to "their country." "Let us hope," cries Bone in a critique of William Gardner Smith's *Last of the Conquerors*, "that it will not be taken as evidence of either Yankee or American chauvinism if we point out that there are in fact important differences between the Negro's status in Philadelphia and in Georgia; between the systematic genocide of the Hitler government and the Supreme Court decision of 1954."

The same "Yankee or American chauvinism" is evidenced in a recent review of *How We Live: Contemporary Life in Contemporary Fiction*, an anthology edited by Penny Chapin Hills and L. Rust Hills. "Of the seven selections devoted to the 'Negro,'" writes the reviewer, Fred Ehrenfeld, "two are by Jews and one by a Southern white writer. The editors feel the need to justify this by contending that there are few good Black writers." Ehrenfeld agrees: "There is truth in this . . . the growing militancy of American Blacks in liberating themselves from their oppression releases energies that must be directed toward political and social ends."

And too, there is Louis Simpson, "a fine contemporary American poet with a liberal and humane sensibility," displaying the degree to which racism has tainted that "sensibility" in a review of a volume of poetry by Pulitzer Prize winner, Gwendolyn Brooks: "I am not sure it is possible for a Negro to write well without making us aware he is a Negro; on the other hand, if being a Negro is the only subject, the writing is not important. . . ."

The star of this Comedy of Errors, however, is Theodore Gross, who contributes the following lines: ". . . every important Negro writer including Malcolm X and Eldridge Cleaver, has been intellectually shaped by a white western tradition. [Malcolm

X, of course, is not an important "Negro writer" since, like Socrates, he had his Plato in Alex Haley] Across all that he has learned —the words, the techniques, the ways of looking at character— fall his own experiences; and the friction of mind and fact creates the special tensions of Negro art. . . . So long as he builds his experiences upon a white western intellectual tradition, the Negro author speaks to whites—intellectually; and he speaks to Negroes —intellectually and empirically."

Gross' statement is applicable only to those Black writers whose obsession to enter the "American Mainstream" is determined by economic and social considerations. For most Black writers, at the present time, such an argument is merely a restatement of the theses propounded by white liberals from Harriet Beecher Stowe to Robert Bone; and constant reiteration in either the social, political, or literary sphere, can only bring us closer to the brink of racial Armageddon.

"I want to be a [writer], not a Negro [writer]." remarked an earlier James Baldwin to Langston Hughes, leading Hughes to comment upon that "urge towards whiteness in the race" which pervaded so much of Black literature in the past. This "urge"— not a belief that he had "been intellectually shaped by a white western tradition"—led the Black writer to dream of mutual estates. Preferring to believe that he could only "build his experiences upon a white western tradition," the writer viewed himself in the mirror of American society and created from his fantasy those characters, images of himself, who accepted a subordinate status in the great American chain of being.

Feigning belief in the mythological American Creed, such writers were imbued with the humanistic rhetoric flowing from the pens and lips of the abolitionists. They were motivated, often by social and economic factors, to function not as Black writers, nor as Black men, but instead as Americans despite tacit recognition of the disparaging difference in culture, history and world view. There were, to be sure, exceptions; men who viewed the world from a realistic perspective, who spoke not to whites but to Blacks, and who introduced the first strain of Black Nationalism into the field of Black literature.

David Walker, author of *The Appeals,* was one such writer;

Martin Delaney, who wrote *Blake or the Huts of Africa*, was another; and Sutton Griggs, who wrote *Imperium In Imperio*, was still another. The first book is a collection of essays, the other two are novels. Despite these differences, they have this in common; they are free of the assimilationist bent of the works of their contemporaries, and each writer, in accepting the political tenets of the Black Nationalist ideology, put forth a formula from which a "Black Aesthetic" could be derived. In circumventing that "urge towards whiteness in the race," they evidenced in their works that concern for separate estates which is such a significant part of the literary and cultural sphere of the Black Power revolution today.

Black writers, having adopted the political dicta of Black Power and, having moved beyond the pioneering position of Walker, Griggs, and Delaney, have set about creating an aesthetic which has its genesis in the nationalism so very apparent in much of Black literature. They have moved toward solving the age old dichotomies between being a Black man and an American and between art and function. Believing with Saunders Redding that "Negroes are different from other Americans; their historical and social position makes this so . . . ," the Black writers of today assert that it is far more important to be a Black writer than an American writer. And believing with Jean Paul Sartre that the serious writer writes not for posterity but for today, they have concluded that literature, to be meaningful, cannot serve as mere artifact, but must instead be functional and relevant to a particular people, a particular era, and a particular place.

Central to this new literary creed is a revolt against the protest novel. Keorapetse William Kgositsile, one of the finest of the young writers, relates in *Negro Digest*: "I do not write protest poetry. My poetry is love poetry. . . . My poetry is that spirit throbbing with the love of millions of Black people all over the world. My stance is racial. . . ."

Kgositsile's observation goes beyond that made by James Baldwin in "Everybody's Protest Novel": ". . . the avowed aim of the American protest novel is to bring greater freedom to the oppressed. [However] The protest novel, so far from being disturbing, is an accepted aspect of the American scene, ramifying that framework we believe to be so necessary." This is true only in regard to protest novels written by Blacks. The novel as a vehicle of protest, when written by whites, has not only disturbed the American scene, but, according to critics like Edmund Wilson, has succeeded in altering it. The failure of the Black protest novel is not in aesthetics, as Gross would have us believe, but in the naive, futile attempts of "the Negro author to speak to whites."

Richard Wright shouted most consistently for white men to listen, and he acknowledged that he wrote not for Blacks who already knew about the conditions and situations which he described, but instead for whites whose knowledge was limited. He wrote *Black Boy* for white liberals not realizing that they would find the facts of his life to be little more than "mundane actualities" which had been "crudely recorded." *Black Boy* needs no defense. As a work of art, it stands that "test of time" which Dr. Johnson, a much more judicious critic than his American counterparts, demanded of a literary work. What is significant, however, is the fact that this autobiography failed in its objective—to rouse the conscience of white America.

Black writers, cognizant of Wright's failure, have moved beyond protest, have ceased appealing to "the conscience of white America," and have begun to explore the culture and lives of Black people in an attempt to delineate not the similarities between Blacks and whites, but the many differences. This leads to that "danger of parochialism" which concerns Gross so much. But the danger is not for Black people whose lives are fraught with dangers of every conceivable kind, but instead for white critics whose skills, shaped in the dusty furnaces of Olympus, are inadequate to deal with literature which seeks to produce, not catharsis for whites, but revelation for Blacks.

The codification of the Black Aesthetic is a first step in this endeavor. Denying the dichotomy between art and function, the Black Aesthetic, derived from the political basis of Black Nationalism, propounds the most simplistic of themes: culture derives from the group experiences of a people, and separate experiences produce separate cultures. That the experiences of Black Americans are distinct from those of white Americans perhaps needs no further justification than William Faulkner's oft-qoted remark that he could not imagine himself to be a Negro for five seconds. These distinct experiences have mandated a distinct language, life style, and world view.

Englishmen and Americans, Winston Churchill is supposed to have said, are divided by a common language. The division is even sharper between Blacks and whites in America. On arriving in America, Black slaves were separated from their countrymen with whom they shared a common tongue. The newcomers were, therefore, forced to devise a means of communication with each other, and, in addition, with the white master and overseer. Two sets of language were necessary. And what seemed a difficult task was accomplished when the slaves intuitively stumbled on an important concept of language, that it is both denotative and connotative. Though speaking in the same tongue to Blacks and whites, the words of the slaves differed not only in meaning, but in the metaphors, symbols, and images which derive from a unique group experience. This is what makes Ralph Ellison's novel *Invisible Man* so incomprehensible to sophisticated white critics, leading Herbert Hill to confess: "In *Invisible Man*, Ellison evokes a world which perhaps only an American Negro can fully apprehend."

In developing a distinct system of communication, Black people also developed distinct life styles. These styles are many and varied, yet all have this in common: they are part of an arsenal of weapons devised by the group to confront Americans in a manner that no white American is forced to confront another; and no better example need be supplied than the wide range of characters in the "Negro Novel." James Weldon Johnson's protagonist in *The Autobiography of an Ex-Coloured Man* chooses assimilation as a way of confronting the society; Sheldon Howard in Saunders Redding's *Stranger and Alone*, chooses resignation; Jake, of Claude McKay's *Home to Harlem*, chooses the hedonism of Epicurus; Bigger Thomas, of Wright's *Native Son*, chooses outright rebellion; and Dr. Bledsoe of *Invisible Man*, chooses guile and deception. These styles are used by every Black man sometime during his lifetime, for each style constitutes part of a unique cultural experience.

There can be little question that the Black man has a distinctive world view. "The white man wakes up in the morning and puts on his suit," declares Charlene Hunter, "the black man puts on his armor." And, indeed, the armor is necessary, for few Blacks any longer succumb to American mythology, and view the American society through the eyes of white liberals, or see a society moving rapidly towards equalitarianism. In short, they no longer have faith in white Americans; they have realized, at long last, that white Americans are the spiritual descendants of that mob which shouted "Give us Barabbas!," choosing not only their savior and redeemer, but providing a metaphor of western civilization—with its concentration camps, its colonial armies, and its hanging trees—which has survived the ages.

The unique language, life style, and world view present a conundrum which the white critic cannot possibly resolve. Serious white critics, such as J. C. Furnas, Nat Hentoff, and Milton Meltzer, have realized this fact, and Charles E. Silberman in the introduction to *Crisis in Black and White,* is unusually honest: "There is a certain arrogance, I suppose, in any white man presuming to generalize . . . about how Negroes think and what they are likely to do. . . ." Others, like Richard Gilman, have arrived at this conclusion belatedly. Still others, like Robert Bone and Theodore Gross, seem destined to remain in purgatory; singing, much like Shelley's nightingale, to cheer their own sweet solitude.

"No one," cries Gross, "seems to question the human credentials of a twentieth century, urbanized American graduate when he evaluates some medieval tract in which the language is different, the country and time are strange, the religion of the author may be alien. . . ." As a justification for continued critiques by white scholars of Black literature, the analogy is inaccurate. To see the work of art as more than artifact demands a critical perspective based on the preconceptions and attitudes which the critic brings to his analysis. Like Johnson, Arnold, and Trilling who brought their personal biases to the fore in judging the works of Grey, Byron, and Dreiser; the twentieth century American graduate will probably reflect an arrogant racial superiority toward medieval subjects and literature. That he will reflect such attitudes toward Black authors and Black literature is a certainty substantiated by numerous historical examples. Subjective criticism is as old as Plato's republic, and to suggest the possibility of a leap from subjective bias to objective appraisal in the racial climate of America is the greatest defect in the argument for "Mutual Estates."

One would hope that white liberals, at this juncture of the twentieth century, would realize this fact and begin to search for ways, not of assimilating Blacks into American society, but instead, of perpetuating those differences between Blacks and whites which mandate two separate societies. This means, for the white scholar, a reevaluation of those values which have brought us all, Black and white, to the present crisis. It means also that Black and white critics, working in their separate spheres, may well help stave off a racial Götterdämmerung.

This advice will be lost upon the Grosses of this world, for America has always been a free society for whites who will, no doubt, continue to hand down pronouncements from the tower of Olympus. But, one thing is certain, the pronouncements will be important only to those who refuse to believe with Richard Wright that: "Each day when you see us black folk upon the dusty land of the farms or upon the hard pavement of the city streets, you usually take us for granted and think you know us, but our history is far stranger than you suspect, and we are not what we seem."

18

CULTURAL NATIONALISM:

THE BLACK NOVELIST

IN AMERICA

*"For the western world holds me in fee
And I can never hope for full release
While to its alien Gods, I bend my knee."*
—CLAUDE McKAY

WE ARE FAMILIAR WITH the quest for Black Power in the political, social, and educational spheres of American life; however, few of us are familiar with the long struggle for Black Power or black nationalism in Afro-American letters. Yet in one important genre, the novel, cultural nationalism has been explored since Martin Delaney's fragment, *Blake or the Huts of America*, written in 1859. This quest—beginning early in black literature when the majority of black folk inhabited the rural areas of America—reached its apex at the time of the Harlem Renaissance when the greatest immigration in American history transformed a rural folk into an urban folk.

The ramifications of this statement cannot be properly appraised without an understanding of the cultural dichotomy which has existed for so long in the black community; and a brief history of the Afro-American novel prior to the Harlem Renaissance is necessary to bring the novel of the city into sharper focus.

Clotel could have been written by any member of the Plantation School of writers, for in *Clotel*, William Wells Brown does not minimize the debt he owes to this school. His characters are equally romantic, his situations equally improbable, and his attribution of angelic qualities to those Afro-Americans who are white in every essential except color is in the best tradition of the

Aryan supremacy mythologists. For Brown, as for his white contemporaries, the standards of beauty and excellence are white in
every aspect.

The case is quite different with Martin Delaney. Delaney seeks
to turn the black novel inward, to deal with the black experience
as distinct, bordering only tangentially on the American experience. And what Frederick Douglass said about Delaney sums up, I
believe, Delaney's attitude toward his race and his characters: "I
wake up every morning and thank God for making me a man,"
wrote Douglass, "Delaney thanks God for making him a black
man."

What is important here is that these two brother abolitionists
viewed the function of black literature in different ways. The
novel for Brown was to be at one and the same time a vehicle for
protest as well as a vehicle for cataloguing the achievements of the
race. Those characters who survived the American racial inferno
were rewarded with the artifacts of Western culture. The major
thesis of the novel was the Horatio Alger motif done in colors of
medium grey.

Delaney too viewed the novel as a vehicle of protest; but even
more as a vehicle for affirming the black identity outside of the
American context. For Delaney black men were transplanted Africans, brought by misfortune to a strange land to sing their songs
before alien Gods. Therefore, these Blacks would have to make
the group journey to identity outside the context of the American melting pot theory.

However, the history of the black novel before the Harlem
Renaissance is almost a complete negation of Delaney's thesis, and
the novel, as seen by Brown, would exist with slight variation for
over fifty years. J. McHenry Jones (*Hearts of Gold*, 1898), Pau-
line Hopkins (*In Contending Forces*, 1900), and Paul Laurence
Dunbar (*The Uncalled*, 1901) pay homage to the assimilationist
motif. The experiences of their characters are shown to vary little
from the experiences of white Americans. They argue, sometimes
nauseatingly so, that the only difference between black Americans and white Americans is the accident of color; and they come
very close to arguing in fiction, as Phyllis Wheatley does in
poetry, that Blacks are little more than reformed savages brought

to the altar of Christianity by the grace of Western civilization.

It is not surprising that such novels use as their setting a rural environment. The rural South is the basis of reference and the romantic machinery of Southern life is a necessity for these writers. Mired in the South and steeped in the rural plantation tradition, these early novels were vehicles for the black middle class in the same manner that the novels of Thomas Dixon and Thomas Nelson Page were vehicles for the Southern white aristocracy.

The break with the rural tradition came when the black novel, following the exodus of black people, came to the city. In the nineteenth century, Blacks poured into the nation's urban areas. They went as far west as California, as far north as Canada; and they settled in the Watts', the Houghs, and the Harlems of America. They came, as W.E.B. DuBois was to note, in search of Canaan, and they were sorely disappointed.

Into urban America, they brought their history, their folklore, their customs, and their anger. They demanded a religion which would suit their needs and their ministers came north to minister to them in a new and different setting. They demanded a social structure based not upon caste and color but upon the brotherhood of one black man with another. The similarities between the injustices, North and South, enabled them to pierce the veil of American mythology; and as a result, they demanded not a literature of manners and gentility, but one which would reflect their hopes, fears and anxieties; a literature which would be as forthright as the Garvey movement in presenting their demands and in helping them to achieve a sense of identity.

Alain Locke best summed up this new mood and its literary implications: "Of all the voluminous literature on the Negro," wrote Professor Locke in the introduction to *The New Negro*, "so much is mere external view and commentary that we may warrantably say that nine-tenths of it is about the Negro rather than of him. . . . We turn, therefore . . . to the elements of truest social portraiture, and discover in the artistic self-expression of the Negro today a new figure on the national canvas. . . ."

The "New Negro" was no longer the stereotype of the

Booker T. Washington era; instead he was the new Negro of the cities who, having deserted the farm, was rapidly becoming industrialized and his earliest and most consistent supporter was the poet Langston Hughes.

"To my mind," wrote Hughes in *The Negro Writer and the Racial Mountain*, "it is the duty of the younger Negro artist to change through the force of his art that old whispering 'I want to be white' hidden in the aspirations of his people to 'why should I want to be white? I am a Negro and beautiful.' "

The spirit of Martin Delaney is revived in the Harlem Renaissance; for black was not only beautiful, but also different and distinct. With the acceptance of this fact the black novelist was forced to move away from romanticism and mythology and deal realistically with a people living, dying, hoping, and hating in the ghettoes of America. A cultural renaissance was in its earliest stages and a new cultural awareness was evident in Afro-American life. The pioneers of the Harlem Renaissance did much to bring about this awareness, and in so doing, called for a commitment to reality which would be echoed by the young black writers of the '60's.

The first black writer to affirm this commitment to reality was a young man who, ten years after the Harlem Renaissance, would write in an article, "A Blueprint for Negro Writing": "The Negro writer who seeks to function within his race as a purposeful agent has a serious responsibility. In order to do justice to his subject matter, in order to depict Negro life in all its manifold and intricate relationships, a deep informed and complexed consciousness is necessary; a consciousness which draws its strength upon the fluid lore of a great people, and molds this lore with the concepts that move and direct the forces of history today. The Negro writer is called upon to do no less than create values by which his race is to struggle, live, and die. . . ." The young man was Richard Wright, and four years later he would write *Native Son*, create Bigger Thomas, and move the black novel to a height of realism which, unfortunately, has not been surpassed to this day.

The plot of *Native Son* centers around Bigger Thomas, an uneducated black youngster, born in a Chicago slum, forced to live in a one room hovel with his mother, sister and brother, and relegated to a life of frustration and futility because of the color of his skin. Given a job as the family chauffeur by Mr. Dalton, a "white liberal" who owns the slums in which he is forced to live, Bigger accidentally murders Mary, the "liberal's" daughter. In addition, Bigger murders his own girl friend, not gratuitously but by design, setting up the interesting angle that he was responsible for only one murder—that of his girl friend—a fact which has no bearing on the outcome of his trial for his life. Caught by the police, Bigger is tried and, despite pleas from his communist lawyer, sentenced to die. He dies without repentance, without atonement for the death of the white girl. The catalyst for the action in *Native Son* is the accidental murder of Mary Dalton.

We should not be swayed by the academic critics who, imbued with the notion that "poetry should not mean but be," have dealt with *Native Son* in terminology more appropriate for dealing with the plastic, not the literary arts. Nor should we be swayed by the pseudo-moralists among us who attempt to find in Bigger Thomas the epitome of man's degradation and inhumanity. Rather, let us put *Native Son* into proper historical perspective, and in so doing, deal with the period of the 1940's when the novel was published.

In Europe, German aggression was well under way. In a short time almost the whole of Europe would come under the sway of a tyranny as vicious as that under which Blacks have lived in this country for over two hundred years. In America, the detention camps which would later house American citizens of Japanese descent would be subjected to persecution and abuse. The paranoiac attacks on the Jewish population of Germany would be reiterated in the propaganda attacks on the Jewish population in America. For Blacks, the journey from South to North would prove to be no more than a journey from one kind of oppression to another. For any sensitive individual living in this tumultuous period, the symbol of man's reality was not the tragic clown, as Ralph Ellison would have us believe, but rather the concentration camp. It is in this concentration camp environment that Bigger Thomas was born.

The validity of Bigger Thomas and the test of his humanity

must be examined in light of the concentration camp metaphor. In so doing we are forced to conclude that the murder of Mary Dalton, at one point so shocking and so senseless, is, when viewed from a different perspective, so cathartic and so necessary. In a world where the concentration camp is man's touchstone for reality, the values by which men live and die are existential ones; and one must create his identity, a sense of his own self-worth, out of the chaos and confusion inherent in living as a victim in a dehumanized world.

We have come a long way from Martin Delaney. Delaney would have settled for black emigration back to Africa, to a place where men, free from arbitrary restrictions, might create their own identities. Richard Wright, on the other hand, would settle for nothing less than a piece of this earth, where men would carve their identity out of violence and despair, thereby transcending the limitations imposed upon them. *Native Son* succeeds in destroying the American myth, in rending to shreds the make-believe world of the romantics, in leaving the American dream in shambles, and, finally, in presenting a portrait of reality which serious black writers who followed would have to confront.

Two of today's most popular black writers have had great difficulty in confronting the reality presented by *Native Son*. Neither has accepted the chaos and violence which the novel presents and neither has accepted Richard Wright's nationalistic formula as the best means for bridging the racial chasm and avoiding racial war.

James Baldwin wavers between the philosophy of assimilationism and that of nationalism unable, until *Blues for Mr. Charlie*, to examine American society in other than personal terms. No writer knows the ghetto or its people better than Baldwin, no one has a clearer insight into the alienation and despair of man in the twentieth century, and yet no writer has failed more miserably in depicting in fiction the plight of urbanized black Americans.

Another Country, his most popular novel, serves as a case in point. The beginning of *Another Country* is to be found in the ending. Here one glimpses the New Society as Baldwin envisions it. At the end of the novel three couples remain: a homosexual couple, a heterosexual couple, and an integrated couple. The emphasis should not be placed upon the makeup of the couples, but instead upon the tolerance each shows toward the differences of the others. In a sense, Baldwin would return us to the Garden of Eden before the fall when Adam and Eve, unconscious of their differences, accepted each other in terms of common humanity.

For Baldwin, however, to tread the road back to innocence entails great difficulty. Man must be created anew, and for the characters of *Another Country*, this implies that one must undergo a fire-baptism in which he either accepts his condition or foregoes it altogether. There is no middle ground. Man accepts himself for what he is and moves forward to reshape the world in his own image or failing to accept himself he attempts self-transcendence which may lead to destruction.

Every man, argues Baldwin, has burdens to bear, and a man is distinguished by how well he stands up under his burden. In *Another Country* the two characters who bear the heaviest burdens are Rufus Scott, black, and Eric Jones, homosexual. Eric survives the end of the novel and emerges as the central figure in the new world. He learns to live with his condition, to accept himself for what he is, and thus he is able to pursue a career, and carry on a meaningful relationship with others. Rufus, on the other hand, cannot rise above his condition. The black skin is, symbolically, his shroud and his inability to shed it subconsciously leads him from poverty to degradation and finally to self-destruction. Unlike Eric, who is free to accept himself as a homosexual, Baldwin implies that Rufus, in accepting himself as a black man, must accept the historical terms of degradation and distortion which circumscribe him: self-hate, self-abnegation, despondency, and frustration leading to vindictive acts toward others. Therefore one is led to believe that, in order to enter paradise, Rufus must discard his blackness altogether. In accepting the myths of American society, Baldwin blames the victim for wearing the Star of David and suggests that for the sake of peace, the victim must thrust aside that which offends the victimizer. What emerges from *Another Country* is a subtle plea for integration which goes far beyond the scope envisioned by the early assimilationists.

Every institution in American society has been designed to substantiate the thesis that to be born black is a sin. This is not so.

The sin is not being born black, but being born into a world in which to attain paradise one must pick up the instruments of war. "The symbol of the twentieth century," wrote Richard Wright, "is the man on the corner with a machine gun." In American society, one reaches the Garden of Innocence not through acquiescing in the destruction of his own heritage and identity but by constructing better machine guns than his enemies, or at least, learning to use them more efficiently. To offer black people a Rufus Scott is to offer a Christ in black face, not withstanding the fact that both Christ and Rufus are doomed to die the death of cowards; and that neither the great society nor the Garden of Eden can be built upon a foundation whose chief architects are cowards.

To move from James Baldwin to Ralph Ellison demands that one clarify his own position in regard to the function of the black writer in American society. Mankind exists in a world where injustice is the norm, where persecution is the measure of man's fidelity to his god, where human life is all too often sacrificed on the altar of power politics. Look upon this world of civilized men and your eyes will never fall upon a land where men are not victimized and persecuted by other men whose only claim to power is that they possess an abundance of the instruments of war. Given such conditions, the job of the writer is to wage total war against injustice; in American society this means that the black writer must wage total war against the American system. This does impose a terrible obligation upon the black writer; yet, persecution and oppression are equally terrible. None should argue with the assertion that the writer must be free to utilize his skill in the way he deems best. However, the same scripture holds true for all men, and in a society where some men are not free, freedom for the writer is based upon an absurdity. The black writer in America can never be free until every Black man is free, and the obligation imposed upon the writer is no more severe than that imposed upon any man whose destiny is inextricably bound to that of his brother.

To wage total war against the American system does not mean that the writer will throw a Molotov cocktail or fire a rifle. (Although the time may come when he may have to do just that.) He has far more powerful weapons at his command and these he must use not only to protest the injustices of the present, but also to attempt to bring about those conditions in the future under which peace might prevail.

Such peace can come only when the last tyrant has disappeared from the earth, when the last hydrogen bomb has been dismantled, when the last concentration camp has been razed to the ground, when the last rifle has been broken, when the last man has been lynched because of his color, when the last patriot has died in defense of his Vietnam, and when the last child has gone to bed hungry for the last time in a world rich in natural resources.

Foremost among black writers today, Ralph Ellison is perhaps the best equipped to analyze the precarious peace upon which the American system rests. There is no writer in America who possesses a finer temperament, none with a more thorough knowledge of black history and culture, and none with more devotion to the perfection of the writer's craft. His *Invisible Man*, is a masterpiece, unsurpassed by those of his contemporaries, white or black, American or European. Having said this, however, one asks certain questions, and these questions inevitably lead one to the conclusion that masterpieces may sometimes be irrelevant to the lives of men and nations. The portrait of the Mona Lisa belongs in a museum; in a concentration camp it would be out of place. Men who live on the edge of desperation are not likely to be enthusiastic about the Mona Lisa or comparable "works of art."

When one begins to examine the theory of the masterpiece, he finds that it was put forth by men who sought to erect a barrier between themselves and other men. Traditionally, works of art were the private property of the aristocracy, and a Reubens or a first edition of Pope, differentiated the haves from the have-nots; in the same manner, poverty and starvation serve a similar function today. The creator of such masterpieces was in turn set off from his brother craftsmen, his nation, and his race, and admitted to the economical, social, and educational elite. However, the black writer can never accept elitism, or a barrier which separates him from other black men. Whether he wills it or not, unless he is very lucky or very white, he is not an individual but part of a group and his fate is mirrored in that of the group's. He is no sophisticated minstrel entertaining the sons and daughters of America's academic establishment, but rather a black artist whose every waking moment is a preparation for war, whose every word is an utterance of defiance, whose every action is calculated to move man towards revolution, and whose every thought centers about the coming conflict. He replaces the formula "art for art's sake," as poet, Don L. Lee, has written, with the humane formula, "art for people's sake," and instead of entertaining black men, he educates them, instead of appealing to their sense of aesthetics, he appeals to their instinct for survival, instead of reminding them of the rewards of heaven, he warns them of the realities of hell. There is no elite in the concentration camp, and the inmates of the camp demand, not funeral dirges, but martial marches.

In the opening pages of *Invisible Man,* the reader encounters the protagonist in an underground cellar. The protagonist relates the story of his life, taking the reader on a picaresque journey characterized by laughter, tragedy, and pathos. At the conclusion of the final episode, the reader is capable of empathizing with the protagonist's commitment to live the life of an underground man. He is, as he relates, an invisible man, a faceless being in a world where the machine is king. His journey is an attempt to impose his consciousness upon the world, to force the world to acknowledge his existence. In the final episode of the novel, the protagonist is mistaken for a criminal, Rhinehart, who has learned to cope with his invisibility by being all things to all men. A world in which Rhinehart is the symbol for every man is an absurdity, and thus the protagonist returns to his underground retreat.

On a more basic level, Ellison's protagonist seeks to force the American system to validate his existence, to grant him recognition not as a black man nor as a white man, but as an American. The fallacy of the white liberal's theory of integration and the fallacy of the argument of *Invisible Man* are the same: that the black American can find his identity only in a metamorphosed society in which the melting pot, having bubbled over, has fused the disparate cultures within and produced a product labeled American. In this analysis, one does not seek to destroy evil but to join forces with it. Like James Baldwin, Ellison wants racial peace and he is willing to purchase it at the expense of negating race and culture.

But the road to racial peace lies not through the negation of one's race and culture but through the affirmation of it. What black men demand from America is not validation of their identity as Americans, which would only assimilate them into the present society, but freedom and justice which would lead to the creation of a new society. If one accepts the argument offered by white liberals that, the concentration camp metaphor of Richard Wright is no longer valid, one must argue concomitantly that the symbol of a black Rhinehart, he who creates and re-creates his identity with each new experience, is invalid in black America where the individual identity cannot exist apart from that of the group.

It is not too far wrong to suggest that Afro-American literature awaits its Whitman and the chances of this Whitman appearing are better today than at any time before. Young black writers for whom the city is home are attempting to create a revolutionary literature which moves beyond Richard Wright. They accept the basic premises of Black Nationalism—that black people are different from other Americans—and they echo Edward Channing in arguing that such differences mandate a different literature. They are reexamining their own culture and finding it rich and diverse. They do not deny the relevance of American history to their lives, but they would not change their history by merging them into one. Unlike the Ralph Ellisons of the world, these young writers would never trade Frederick Douglass for a Thomas Jefferson for they know that one was a slaveholder and the other a crusader against slavery and that, in such an exchange, they would get the short end of the bargain.

They are such men as Ed Bullins in drama, LeRoi Jones in poetry, and John Williams in fiction; and though I have spoken of them as new, their spirit is not new at all. It is the spirit exemplified by Martin Delaney, Walt Whitman and Richard Wright. And each has this in common; he realizes with Nietzsche that the old tables of the law have led us to corruption and oppression and must therefore be replaced by new ones. But more important, in adopting the tenets of Black Nationalism, he realizes with James Joyce that the writer can have no greater task than "to forge from the smithy of his soul, the uncreated conscious of the race."

19

REVOLUTIONARY PHILOSOPHY:

THREE BLACK WRITERS

"Every intellectual," writes Ignazio Silone, "is a revolutionary." We in the black community know from empirical evidence that this is not so. We do know, however, that every reformer is a potential revolutionary, for revolution begins when reform proves to be impossible. The reformer is the prophet of the possible; he has unlimited faith in manmade institutions. He believes in the just society and that events will bring it into being. He dedicates himself to a future world ordained not by man but by God and time, and thus he is not outside of history but history's captive. Like Abraham, to quote Auerbach, "his soul is torn between desperate rebellion and hopeful expectation."

The moment arrives when this inner dichotomy is resolved, when the forces of "desperate rebellion" take possession of his soul. When this occurs, he breaks his pact with history, steps outside of it, becomes a proponent of the impossible, an outlaw; which is to say, he becomes a revolutionary.

There was Frederick Douglass, the young man who began as a disciple of William Lloyd Garrison in 1841 and became the voice of the abolitionist movement. He is not the same Douglass we meet ten years later. The earlier Douglass was a reformer, dedicated to bringing into being "the community of man." He advocated moral suasion, a program designed not to kill the master, but to transform him, and by so doing, to transform the society. The later Douglass, however, began to realize that the only justification for moral suasion is faith in history—an unsure faith, for history can sanction either justice or injustice. He therefore chose to step outside of history, to dedicate himself to the proposition that the master must die, that the old institutions must be gutted by fire, not eroded by time, and a new moral code created out of the ashes of the old. It is thus that he champions old John Brown, American history's first white outlaw who, with a bible in one hand and a rifle in the other, pledged himself to revolution.

There were the freedom riders of the nineteen-sixties, reformers who dared not call for the maximum—destruction of the existing social order—being denied the minimum decency, dignity, and justice, brooding like Douglass, going back to their colleges bruised, battered, jail-weary and contemplating the step across the boundary line which separates reform from revolution.

There was Martin Luther King, dedicated to the things of the spirit, standing atop the mountain, saddened by the reluctance of his country to grant minimum reforms and thus make revolution unnecessary.

For if the minimum is impossible to achieve, why should men not dedicate themselves to securing the maximum? If Satan cannot gain a small part of heaven by petition, why not attempt to take all of heaven at the point of a gun? If societies are unwilling to accept the formula "some if not all," why should men not embrace the absolutionist formula of Ivan Karamazov, "all or none." To such questions, the answer of the black reformer is as positive as that of Frederick Douglass. The black man who began as a reformer, pledging himself to some if not all, becomes a revolutionary, pledging himself to all or none. In so doing, he takes the first fateful step outside of American history, moving away from the influence of the gradualists and the integrationists, becoming an outlaw, one who seeks not only to create the new society, but also a new morality which will produce, to use Julius Lester's phrase, "the new man."

"He taught us nothing," Matthew Arnold wrote of Lord Byron in the nineteenth century, "but our soul has felt him like the thunderer's roar." We too, have our hero in the twentieth century, but unlike Byron, not only have we felt him in the deepest part of our souls, but he has also taught us a great deal. Martin Luther King was the apostle of reform and in his living and dying, he taught us that reform in American society is impossible. He taught us that the problem of the twentieth century is no longer, as DuBois believed at the beginning of the century, the problem of the color line, for such is not a problem but a conundrum and incapable of solution. The problem is whether black men will attempt a revolution based upon the highest tenets of morality—justice, brotherhood, and individual worth, or conform to American history by attempting a revolution based upon nihilism or gangsterism.

The society which crucifies the reformer and the revolutionary on the same cross makes reform impossible and violence inevitable. The sum total of King's non-violent life and his violent death reduces the options of black Americans to two: revolution or nihilism; and even as the cortege follows his body to its final resting place, the chaos and confusion following his death tips the scale in favor of nihilism. The man who bore the cross as a shield is discovered to have had a less powerful weapon than the gun; thus the instrument of Martin Luther King's destruction becomes the symbol of the black man's salvation. The stage is set for vengeance and redemption and upon this stage, gun in hand, the philosopher of nihilism appears.

"During my last stay in prison," writes Eldridge Cleaver, "I made the desperate decision to abandon completely the criminal path and to redirect my life." The new direction led to the publication of two books, *Soul On Ice* and *Eldridge Cleaver*, a position as Minister of Information of the Black Panther Party, and a presidential candidacy on the slate of the Peace and Freedom Party in 1968.

Today Cleaver is hunted by a government whose morality is inferior to his. Even the crime of rape which sent him to so many prisons, San Quentin, Folsom, Soledad, pales into insignificance when measured alongside the rape perpetrated by the United States Government, with the sanction of the American people, upon half the world. However, similarities between hunted and hunter are so great as to approach the height of irony. Cleaver is the American society in microcosm, a pragmatist whose years in prison have taught him how this "world goes." More so than any other man in the last 50 years he has stripped America of her facade, removed the tinsel and symbolized in his own person what she is now and has always been. The nation which traded the cross for the gun, now hunts a man who, gleefully, without embarrassment, welcomes the exchange.

In this context *Soul On Ice* becomes more than a personal document; its ramifications extend the width and breadth of America. For what comprises reality for the average American if not the belief that the world evolves around muscle, that at the apex of the universe is the gun, that American morality rests upon power, and that in America, as nowhere else, gangsterism is idealism pushed to actuality? Cleaver, in two essays in his first book, reveals his kinship with these "average Americans." In the first, "Notes On A Native Son," a vicious, unwarranted attack upon James Baldwin, one must dig deep for Cleaver's central thesis. This thesis is not James Baldwin's ambiguity concerning his racial identity. What annoys Cleaver, and occasions the essay, is the presence of homosexuality in a world ruled by "Supermasculine Menials." "Baldwin," writes Cleaver, "despised not Richard Wright, but his masculinity." For Cleaver as for America, masculinity, the essence of brute force, is the symbol of power. Those who wield the rifles or bang down the guillotine must be men with all the connotations the term implies in a masculine oriented society.

A "student of Norman Mailer's 'The White Negro,'" Cleaver, like Mailer, asks us to journey back to the days of Neanderthal Man, to the noble savage whose most important characteristic was his toughness. Here among mankind's first gangsters, manhood is measured by the savagery each man displays towards the others. In this environment, Bigger Thomas becomes for Cleaver what he was not for Richard Wright, a glorified gangster seeking to wreak revenge upon a society in which brute force is the norm. The man who begins by raping people, argues William Strickland, ends by raping society.

Cleaver's thesis, although symbolic and metaphorical, is nevertheless more clearly stated in the essay, "The Primeval Mitosis." The debt to Mailer is still being paid. Society is torn apart by two opposing forces symbolic of the dual aspects of man's nature. The higher instincts, those of the mind, are characterized by the Omnipotent Administrator; man's basic, primeval instincts, those of the body, are characterized by the Supermasculine Menials. "Weakness, frailty, cowardice, and effeminancy are, among other attributes, associated with the mind. Strength, brute power, force, virility, and physical beauty are associated with the body." Those who told us that the weak would inherit the earth are here revealed for the liars that they are. The world, according to Cleaver, belongs to the Supermasculine Menials.

In "The Land Question and Black Liberation," the central essay in *Eldridge Cleaver*, the role of the Supermasculine Menials in the early stages of the revolution is clear: they will guide us to the first way station on the road to *Götterdämerung*. "The violent phase of the black liberation struggle is here, and it will spread . . . America will be painted red. Dead bodies will litter the streets and the scene will be reminiscent of the disgusting, terrifying, nightmarish news reports coming out of Algeria during the height of the general violence."

In this orgy of violence, however, we are comforted by the fact that we do not fight Goliath alone: "Not only would black people resist, with the help of white people, but we would also have the help of those around the world who are just waiting for some kind of extreme crisis within this country so that they can move for their own liberation from American repression abroad."

[I stood, jolted by the naiveté of my father who refused to admit to himself that the white communists had sold him and his people down the river, that when the chips were down they had settled for Soviet-Communist unity rather than continue to confront oppression of Blacks in America. I am jolted too, here, twenty-five years later, when history is not only so blatantly ignored but discarded as irrelevant. The history of whites in this country—farmers of Tom Watson's day, communists of the days of my father, and liberals of Martin Luther King's day—has been that when the decision must be made between life and death, between stability and chaos, few have been willing, to quote Albert Camus, "to go to the bitter end." The concentration camp is a lonely, deadly place; and few whites have ever been willing to embrace Blacks there.]

Eldridge Cleaver, metaphor of American society, has accepted the moral formula of America's madmen—an eye for an eye—and proposed to deal with the madmen on their terms. Neither reformer nor revolutionary, he is a prophet of the apocalypse, telling us not what we are destined to become but what we are. When he accepts the American reality for his own, when he chooses to champion the forces of American history instead of opposing them, when he accepts the gun and the world of the gun as the essential reality, he ceases to be an outlaw, and becomes what is infinitely worse, more American than the Americans.

The problem is not Cleaver's alone. It is endemic to the whole black revolution and occasioned by men who, frustrated in personal life, seize upon the black revolution as a cathartic exercise. The serious black revolutionary has no conflict between mind and body. The conflict is a much more severe one. The most schizoid of men, he is destined never to be a whole man, to always be many men, forced to operate "upon two planes of reality." He must be aware of Cleaver's major thesis, that the American society is one of the gun and that it evolves around muscle and brute force. However, for him, this constitutes only one aspect of reality, never the ultimate, a dedication to which means to be dedicated to insanity.

It is incumbent upon him to believe that the opposite reality is equally true: that men are more the victims of systems than the originators of them, that no man is inherently evil, and that somewhere in the netherworld of man's psyche there exists a human being like himself. Based upon these two conflicting aspects of reality, the revolutionary sanctions the use of the gun while at the same time deploring its use, argues for violence while hating the necessity for it, wages war while declaring that all war is illegitimate. The essential justification for the black revolutionary is to make black people better than they are.

To make black people better than they are would be a revolution in itself. The major characteristic of past revolutions is that each has become a carbon copy of the system it displaced. The revolutionary who begins by attacking corruption and abuse and demanding "all power to the people" soon discovers that the people are no more virtuous, no more moral, no more willing to exercise power judiciously than the culprits who were overthrown.

This naive, romantic belief in the virtue of the people has had serious repercussions for black revolutionaries of the past. The failures of the rebellions of Denmark Vesey, Nat Turner, and Gabriel Prosser, and the decline of the Garvey movement can be traced to the betrayal of one black man by another. Today, the infiltration of many black nationalist organizations by agents of the city, state, and federal governments is made possible by a simple faith born out of a frustrated desire to regard all black men as seekers after change.

What, then, would it mean to substitute hell for heaven when both are ruled by the same tyrant? The acquisition of a separate paradise, if possible, given the expropriation by Blacks of the worst characteristics of whites—greed, lust, and hypocrisy—would demand that the black revolutionary once again strap his carbine about his shoulders. Before the phrase "power to the people" has any meaning beyond the metaphysical, the people must undergo a metamorphosis, must be cleansed of their Americanism, must become "new men." "Man," wrote the German philosopher, Friedrich Nietzsche, "is a link between the ape and the superman"; the Negro is a link between the slave and the new man; he is something that must be surpassed.

At this point, the black revolutionary lays down his rifle, conscious that an important task awaits him. He who masters the gun is as important as the gun itself; for like a fickle woman, the gun does the bidding of tyrants and revolutionaries alike. The revolution which moved beyond reformism, denounced non-violence, and made the gun a part of the consciousness of black people, turns now to black people themselves to make them conscious of their past, of their historical value, and lays the cultural foundation from which the moral revolution must spring. In the shadow of the holocaust, we turn from the world of emotion to the world of reason, from the world of the primitive to the world of enlightened man. We travel but a few steps from the prophet of nihilism and we encounter the prophet of cultural revolution.

Like Eldridge Cleaver, Harold Cruse is the author of two books, *The Crisis of the Negro Intellectual* and *Revolution or Rebellion*. And like Cleaver, Cruse had little formal education. That Cruse did not get lost in a sterile, academic atmosphere was perhaps for the better, when one realizes the extensive education he acquired on his own. His post-secondary school education was gained through serving in the United States Army during World War II travelling from one point on the globe to another, digesting books in the libraries, or in the lonely solitude of a small room, and finally through membership in the Communist Party.

An intellectual, whose mind has been formed in the day to day world and heightened by contact with the minds of scholars, past and present, Cruse has a unique vantage point from which to peer down on his fellow black intellectuals. His vision is too often clouded, especially in *The Crisis of the Negro Intellectual,* with personal invective, acrimonious insults, insignificant attacks upon insignificant figures, and an ego problem which would delight Freudians everywhere. However, when brought to bear directly upon the racial situation in America, his vision concerning the crisis of the black intellectual is crystal clear. The crisis is one of soul. Having bartered away parts of his soul to numerous American Mephistophleles—Jews, white liberals, capitalists, and communists—the black intellectual can become master of his soul once again only by acquiring complete mastery over his own cultural apparatus: "The path to the ethnic decentralization of American Society is through its culture, that is to say through its cultural apparatus, which comprises the eyes, ears, and the mind of capitalism and its twentieth century voice to the world."

In other words, the crisis can be resolved only when men, searching for their identities, delve deep into their past, attempt to find out from whence they have come. To move outside of American history, men must plunge into their past, sift through the centuries of lies and distortions, and be born again, not in the American image, but in that of their ancestors. In fact, not fiction, Cruse heralds the coming of the "new Negro," the breaker of icons, the smasher of "the old tables of the law," the remaker of men and societies.

"The Black revolt is as palpable in letters as it is in the streets

. . ." writes Hoyt Fuller; and this revolt is being carried on not by the Supermasculine Menials, but by cultural scholars and analysts. For concurrent with the "war in the streets" is a cultural war waged not only for men's minds but for their souls as well. To return to the black past, to forge a momentary concordat with history, is to renew one's forces for the final confrontation. Somewhere between the landing of the first slave ship and Reconstruction, the past of black people was stolen away, much as Prometheus stole the sacred fire from Olympus and the attempt to regain that past has been frustrated by more powerful, less moral gods than Prometheus': Black intellectuals, integrationists, and white liberals.

To regain this past, men must look beyond the gun to ". . . the new concept of cultural revolution." In *Rebellion or Revolution*, Cruse writes: "We maintain that this concept affords the intellectual means, the conceptual framework, the theoretical link that ties together all the disparate conflicting and contending trends within the Negro movement as a whole in order to transform the movement from a mere rebellion into a revolutionary movement that can shape ideas to fit the world into a theoretical frame."

So far have we come from the year 1906 in which the architects of the N.A.A.C.P., plotting their skirmish with American Society, enunciated a platform whose major planks may be reduced to two: the reformation of American Society, wherein the Constitution would be applicable to all citizens of the republic, and an extension of the Booker T. Washington program of racial uplift, a program with the ostensible purpose of making black people worthy of the benefits gained as a result of reform. The first plank was burned to ashes by the fiery rhetoric of Eldridge Cleaver who is after all merely the antithesis of Roy Wilkins. The other falls apart under the careful analysis of Harold Cruse.

Cruse asks us to step back from the confrontation, to pause, to take stock of ourselves, to reinvest ourselves with the verities of old, to wage cultural war and in so doing, produce the new man and the true revolutionary. We are called to an intellectual awakening where the intellectual, having resolved the crisis of identity, becomes "nationalistic in terms of the ethnic and cultural attributes of his art expression." The men who return to pick up the gun differ from those who put it aside. Out of the clay of nationalism, a black man is born anew, dedicated to revolution instead of nihilism. In making the existential leap outside of American history, he has ceased to be its captive; in gaining mastery of himself, he has ceased to be the servant of the gun, but vice versa. Realizing now that guns without moral sanctions become instruments of destruction not salvation, he moves further along the path which divides nihilism from revolution, and there, at the crossroads, extending his hand in greeting, is the prophet of moral revolution.

In the third of three books, *Revolutionary Notes*, Julius Lester writes: "The revolutionary must seize upon experience as an opportunity to make himself more revolutionary, to make himself more the new man. The revolutionary's commitment is not to the destruction of the dehumanizing system . . . the destruction of the dehumanizing system is only a prelude to the creation of conditions under which man may be fulfilled. Even as the revolutionary plans his attack upon the dehumanizing system, he keeps at the core of his being, not the destroying, but the creating that must follow . . . We must destroy in order to live, but let us never enjoy the destroying more than the New Life, the only reason for the destroying."

The revolutionary must always wage war with the madman inside of himself. In American society where gangsterism is all pervasive, each man begins adult life as a gangster. What distinguishes the revolutionary from other men is that he is committed to discarding the gangsterism in his makeup. Too often in America, the tendency has been to define black revolutionaries in American terminology. Thus the difference between a black revolutionary and a black reformer was said to hinge upon the devotion of one to violence and the other to non-violence.

To devote oneself to non-violence, however, means to surrender to gangsterism, to lie impotent before the massive roll of the juggernaut of American history. To dedicate oneself to violence without the restraining influence of a moral code is to acquiesce in terror, and to champion the extension of the history of American oppression from the United States to Vietnam. As the black revolution borders upon gangsterism, moves closer to defining it-self in terms of American history, Julius Lester imparts a moral note, attempts to establish a golden mean. From confrontations with the racist structure in Mississippi, from living among the people of the Delta, working with them, sleeping with them, and fighting with them, Lester has carved out "of those most terrify-ing of Southern nights," a philosophy which calls black men to the noblest of all endeavors—the creation of a new social order.

The philosophy takes shape in his first book, *Look Out Whitey, Black Power's Gon Get Your Momma*, and reaches ma-ture form in *Revolutionary Notes*. In the first book, Lester, anal-ogous to Cruse, councils the black artist: "The artist is essentially a revolutionary whose aim is to change people's lives. He wants people to live better and one way of doing it is to make them see, hear, and feel what he has seen, heard, and felt. The artist is not concerned with beauty, but with making man's life better."

In *Revolutionary Notes*, the message, amplified, becomes one for all men: "But many blacks see the struggle as black against white. Perhaps it is, but if that is true, then nothing really matters. It is not enough to love black people and hate white people. That is therapy, not revolution. It is incumbent upon the revolu-tionary that he not do to someone else what that someone may have done to him. . . . The revolutionary is he who loves humanity and hates injustice. It is only through a commitment of this kind that social change in America will result in revolution and not in another of the varieties of oppression."

Julius Lester is a good man, and like all good men he asks us to be better than we are, to follow him outside of American history, outside of a nation which places a higher value upon material things than it does upon human life, which awards a higher honor to the hypocrite and the military murderer than to the priest and scribe. As we move forward towards Armageddon, Lester asks us to transcend gangsterism, to remember that the gun is merely a necessary instrument to be discarded once and for all when new men, having created a new morality, have brought the new society into existence.

"You black militants," remarked a colleague, "are incurable dreamers." Perhaps we are! We began as slaves outside of American history and we dissipated two hundred years of energy attempting to get inside, unaware that we were seeking to ally ourselves with evil. In 1965, Stokely Carmichael cast himself against the tide of American history, removed himself from the back of the diseased tiger, and many of us followed him. When we did so, we began to dream dreams different from those of our fathers. We dreamed not of integration but of nationalism, not of a melting pot theory but of a pluralistic theory, not of a great society but of a new one. More important, we dreamed of fashioning Canaan out of the debris of the American society, of erecting a nation predicated not upon the gun but upon morality, and if these dreams are hopeless, then so too is the future of mankind. We do not believe that they are hopeless. At this point of the twentieth century in this land of gangsterism, we remain committed to the proposition that man's highest allegiance is to man, that a new world is ours to construct, and amidst the roar of the bombs of hate and dissension, with Margaret Walker, we intone: "Let a new earth arise. Let another world be born. Let a bloody peace be written in the sky. Let a second generation full of courage issue forth, let a people loving freedom come to growth, let a beauty full of healing and a strength of final clenching be the pulsing in our spirits and our blood. Let the martial songs be written, let the dirges disappear. Let a race of men now rise and take control."

DATE DUE

AP 30 '93			
GAYLORD			PRINTED IN U.S.A.